The Huzur Vadisi Vegetarian Cookbook

Recipes from a Turkish kitchen
by Jane Worrall

Copyright © Jane Worrall 2012

Photography
Julia Coulson
Gordon and Jan Crabb
Saskia van Osnabrugge

Design
Tim Beckham - bkmdesignstudio.co.uk

CONTENTS

PREFACE — 5
INGREDIENTS — 8
RECIPES

SOUPS — 13
SALADS and APPETISERS — 21
MAIN DISHES — 39
EGG DISHES — 51
PASTA DISHES — 55
DESSERTS — 67

INDEX — 71

All recipe quantities are to serve four

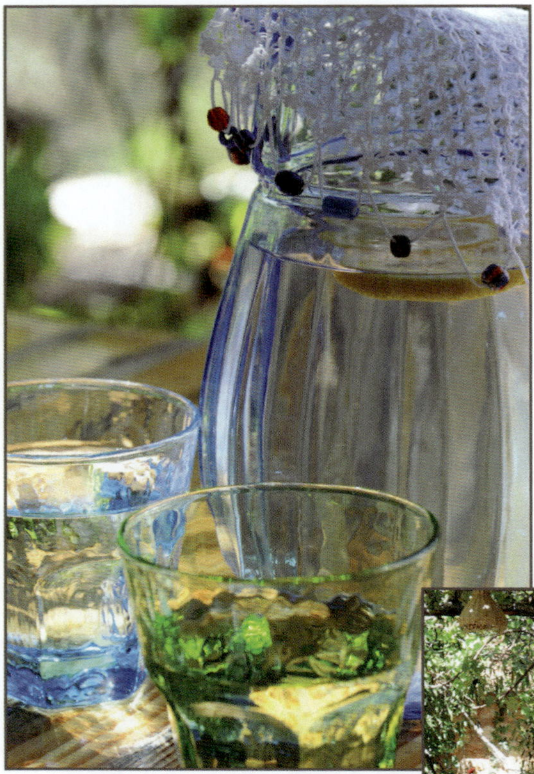
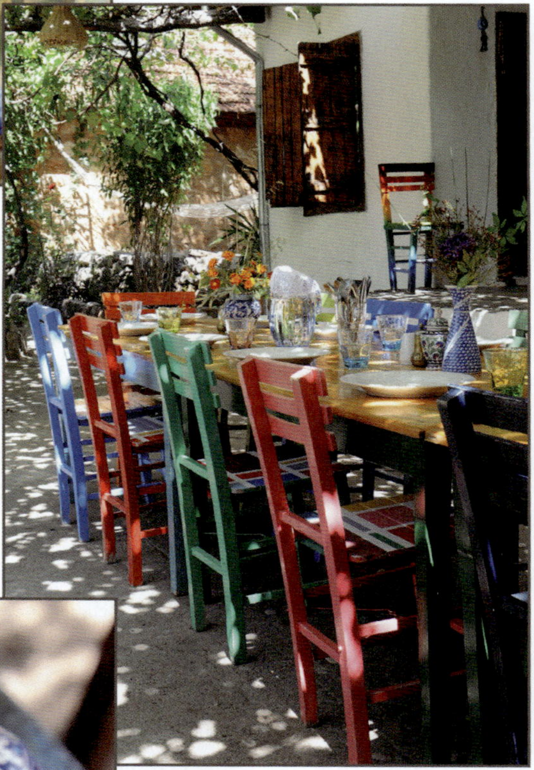
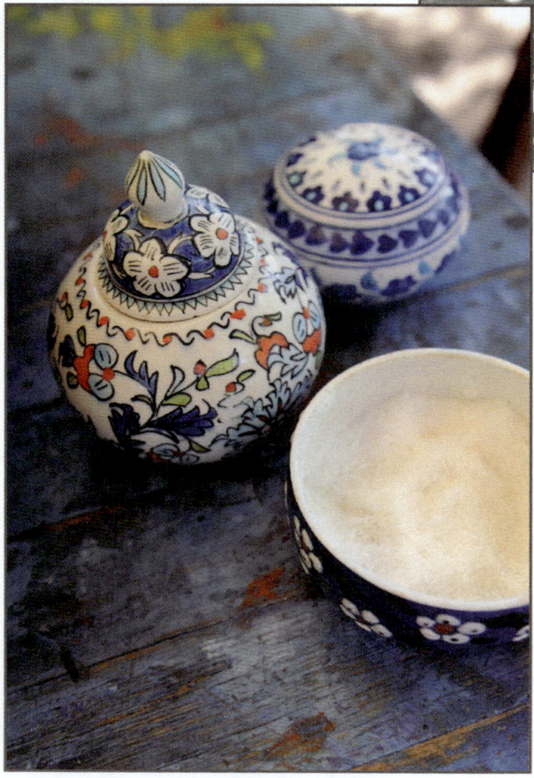

PREFACE

Huzur Vadisi

It goes without saying that one of the important features of a holiday is the food. Over the past fifteen years our guests have been telling us that the food at Huzur Vadisi is so good that we ought to write a cookery book – we even earned a quote from Harpers & Queen magazine calling our food 'legendary'. So at long last here it is!

Huzur Vadisi is an olive farm in the mountains of southwest Turkey. It has been in my ex-husband's family for generations, but had stood empty for twenty years before we acquired it with the idea of creating a holistic holiday centre. It could be said the story began over forty years ago when my brother, Ian, and I came to live in Istanbul as children. In 1993 we formed a partnership and returned to Turkey, the land of our childhood. We wanted to create an alternative to the tourism that destroys the very thing that visitors come to enjoy and we were concerned that the Turkey we knew and loved was under threat from the growing tourist industry.

We met Tanfer Taka, who shared our ideals of a sustainable, community based tourism venture and he became our business partner.

Initially we searched along the Mediterranean coast, from Dalaman to Antalya, for the perfect spot to realise our dream, until one day Tanfer brought us to see his grandfather's land near Göcek. We were enchanted by the utter peace, the wind in the pine forest – and at night not a light to intrude upon the blackness and starlight. When we first came to Huzur Vadisi the terrace walls had crumbled, the house was derelict, the roof full of holes and the rooms had been used for animals and grain storage. We began to put it back together; constructing accommodation in traditional nomadic yurts; excavating a swimming pool; planting gardens; and tending the olive trees which yield the fragrant golden oil used in the kitchen. We now cater for up to thirty guests a week who come on yoga holidays. The atmosphere we try to create is of being a houseguest, and people do tell us that they feel as if they are visiting friends. They also feel drawn into the local community, with whom we have close links.

The three partners, Jane, Ian and Tanfer

Part of the experience is the local village cuisine, which is simple, delicious and healthy. Our star turn in the kitchen is Sevgi, Tanfer's sister. She is not a professionally trained chef, but like all Turkish women she learned at her mother's knee how to chop, peel and prepare food with astonishing flair and dexterity. Without turning a hair and without apparent haste, she can turn out a three-course meal for thirty guests. Her cuisine is based on local village specialities, which give her dishes a wonderful home cooked quality, all freshly prepared for each meal from local ingredients, but also including many traditional recipes from the broader spectrum of Turkish cuisine.

Sevgi and assistant cook, Kublay

Turkish Cuisine

Knowledge of Turkish cuisine often tends to be limited to the ubiquitous döner kebab, which is a bit like judging British food by its fish and chips. What is not so well known is that Turkish cuisine is rated as one of the three great cuisines of the world, along with French and Chinese. The story of its development is unique as much of it was created to tempt the palate of one individual, Allah's representative on earth, the Sultan of the Ottoman Empire.

Originally a nomadic people from the Central Asian steppes, the Turks began to conquer Asia Minor, modern day Turkey, nearly a thousand years ago. They brought their own dishes, yogurt, kebabs, pastry parcels called börek, and like Marco Polo in later years, noodles (or pasta) from north-western China, where Turkish is still spoken. A ravioli type dish called manti is one of Turkey's most traditional dishes and is served with garlic yogurt. Over the centuries these traditional nomadic dishes were added to and refined at the Ottoman Sultan's court.

During the five hundred years of the Ottoman Empire, Turkey's dominions extended from North Africa, Persia, and the Middle East to the Balkans and Greece. During this period the Sultan's chefs in the great palace of Topkapi in Istanbul devoted themselves to creating a sumptuous cuisine, which was unrivalled in history, and which forms the basis of Turkish cuisine today. At the height of the period over one thousand chefs were employed to tempt and delight the Sultan's palate – a fairy tale of oriental sensuality.

The chefs drew on all the resources at their disposal, from the influences of the great civilisations that had occupied the land, the Hittites, the Byzantines, the Greeks, and Seljuk Turks to the geographical benefits of a long coastline and varied topography that supplies a huge range of produce. The dishes created at the Sultan's court can now be found throughout the countries that were formerly in the Empire – kebabs, pilav, aubergine delicacies, feta cheese, dolmas (stuffed vegetables) and of course the sticky, nutty pastries like baklava.

Given this pedigree it is no surprise that visitors to Turkey are delighted at the epicurean pleasures they find there. Over the centuries the Turks have developed a discerning palate, and this includes even simple households, who are connoisseurs of everything from local specialties to the relative merits of different drinking waters. The setting of the meal is also very important, and people will go out of their way to eat at a restaurant set by running water or in a flowery garden. The Turks are also the original picnic people – perhaps harking back to their nomadic roots. There's nothing they like better than a little al fresco dining – and you can forget the sandwiches. Picnics are often as sumptuous as a meal at home with salads, cheeses, dips, stuffed vegetables.

Meals are also still very much the focus of Turkish family and social life, the hit and run style of eating has yet to make substantial inroads, and great care is taken over the preparation. In the villages particularly, cooking is still the woman's domain. However, in this fairly traditional society you will find most professional chefs are men.

Every region has its different specialties, ranging from the spicy oven baked foods of the east, to the Mediterranean and Aegean where olive oil is used to prepare many delicious vegetable and meat dishes.

Sevgi's Cooking

Sevgi's cooking at Huzur Vadisi tends to reflect all these influences, plus adds a dimension of local village specialities, particularly as cooked in the home by women. For this reason the dishes are a little different to what you may find in a restaurant, although some of the traditional Ottoman dishes are the same.

We wouldn't claim that we represent the infinite variety that was the result of the Ottoman sultans' kitchen staff toiling to create exquisite dishes to tempt the Sultan's palate, but we did have a guest 'complain' once that in a two week holiday he hadn't had the same dish twice.

Vegetarian diet

Turkish village cooking is mainly vegetarian, which comes as something of a surprise to many people. This has developed mainly due to necessity. To slaughter a valuable animal which may be kept for its milk as much as its meat, and would be too large for a family to consume, has resulted in meat only being eaten on special occasions.

As a result, the Turkish village diet could have been designed by a nutritionist – the staples are fresh vegetables, salads, fruit, pulses, grains, seeds, rice, olive oil, yogurt, cheese, nuts and dried fruit.

I have cooked the recipes in this book in our kitchen in Wales – so they do transfer, and are possible even if you are not a Turkish master chef. Enjoy!

Jane Worrall

Sevgi's Cooking

ADNAN
AKYOL
Zeytinleri
Siyah Zeytin
ADNAN
AKYOL
Zeytinleri

INGREDIENTS

Most of the ingredients used in these recipes are the sort of things you can easily find at the green grocers or supermarket, with one or two exceptions, for which there are readily available substitutes.

Beans and peas

Pulses are widely used in Turkish cookery, both fresh and dried. To use the dried variety, soak them overnight in cold water, discarding the water the next day before cooking as instructed in the recipe. A quicker way is to pour on boiling water and leave the beans to soak for an hour before cooking. You can of course use tinned beans, which are even quicker. When cooking at home I always use tins and find them perfectly good.

Red pepper flakes (Pul Biber)

One ingredient that is quite specific, which you can buy if visiting Turkey, or are lucky enough to live near a Turkish or Middle Eastern grocery, is pul biber, or red pepper flakes. These come in sweet and hot varieties, and have a particular flavour, which adds to the dish. If you can't get your hands on any pul biber then a mixture of chilli and paprika are a good substitute.

Yogurt

Yogurt is Turkey's gift to the world. First discovered and used by the Turks' nomadic ancestors, it is a tremendously valuable addition to the modern diet, containing the bacterial cultures necessary for health in the digestive tract. It is also a staple of the modern Turkish diet. Nearly every meal is accompanied by a yogurt dish of some sort. In these recipes try to use a live natural yogurt that has a tang to it, rather than the creamy dessert type.

Tomatoes

In Turkey fresh tomatoes are always used in recipes, but you can substitute these with the tinned variety, if you prefer. In some ways the tinned variety are preferable as fresh tomatoes in Britain rarely have the taste you find in Turkish field tomatoes. If you decide to use fresh, to remove the skins place the tomatoes in boiling water for 30 seconds, remove with a slotted spoon and place in cold water. You can then easily remove the skins with a sharp knife.

Filo Pastry

The wafer thin rounds of dough known as filo pastry are widely available in supermarkets and Middle Eastern groceries. It is used in a whole range of Turkish cooking, both savoury and sweet.

Feta Cheese

Turkish white cheese (beyaz peynir) is a sheep or goats milk cheese (although increasingly it is made from cows milk), which is the same as the well-known Greek feta cheese. It can be quite salty, (this can vary) and if you want to remove some of the salt before using it, cut it into chunks and soak for 20 minutes in warm water.

Tahini

Tahini is a paste made from ground sesame seeds, available from supermarkets and health food shops. There is a light and dark variety, the dark being roasted seeds. In Turkish cookery the light version is always used, and is a nutritious addition to many dishes, including hummus.

Pine Nuts

These small pale yellow nuts are usually lightly browned in butter or olive oil before being added to recipes. They add a nutty texture to rice dishes, stuffings and desserts. As they are quite expensive they are often replaced in rice dishes by spaghetti broken into small pieces, lightly browned in the same way before adding the rice and water. A small pine nut shaped pasta called şehriye is used in Turkey.

Dried Mint

Mint is another important ingredient in Turkish cooking, and is nearly always used in the dried form. If you can get this from a Middle Eastern grocery it will be more pungent than the usual supermarket variety.

Green peppers

In Turkey green peppers come in a long, pale green variety that are used in salads and cooking. Bell peppers are used for stuffing. If you can't find the long variety, bell peppers can be substituted.

Aubergines

Turkish cookery should have the sub-title '101 ways with Aubergines', as it is used in so many imaginative and delicious ways. It is often recommended to place the sliced aubergine in a bowl, sprinkling liberally with salt, covering with cold water and setting aside for 30 minutes. It is then rinsed and patted dry on kitchen roll. This allegedly draws out slightly bitter juices. However, I have to say that I often don't bother with this rigmarole and haven't noticed much difference.

Parsley

Parsley in Turkish recipes is always the flat leafed Italian type parsley, which has a distinctive pungent flavour.

Rice

For rice dishes I recommend Basmati rice, which has an aromatic nutty flavour and is delicious enough to be eaten by itself when prepared in the Turkish way.

Bulgur

Another staple ingredient in Turkish village cooking is bulgur, or cracked wheat, which is available from supermarkets and wholefood stores.

Olive oil

You should always use the best olive oil you can, as it is an important addition to the flavour of the dish. Cold pressed oil is best.

Organic

Most of the ingredients at Huzur Vadisi are very fresh and mainly organic, which adds considerably to the flavour, so you might like to use organic produce.

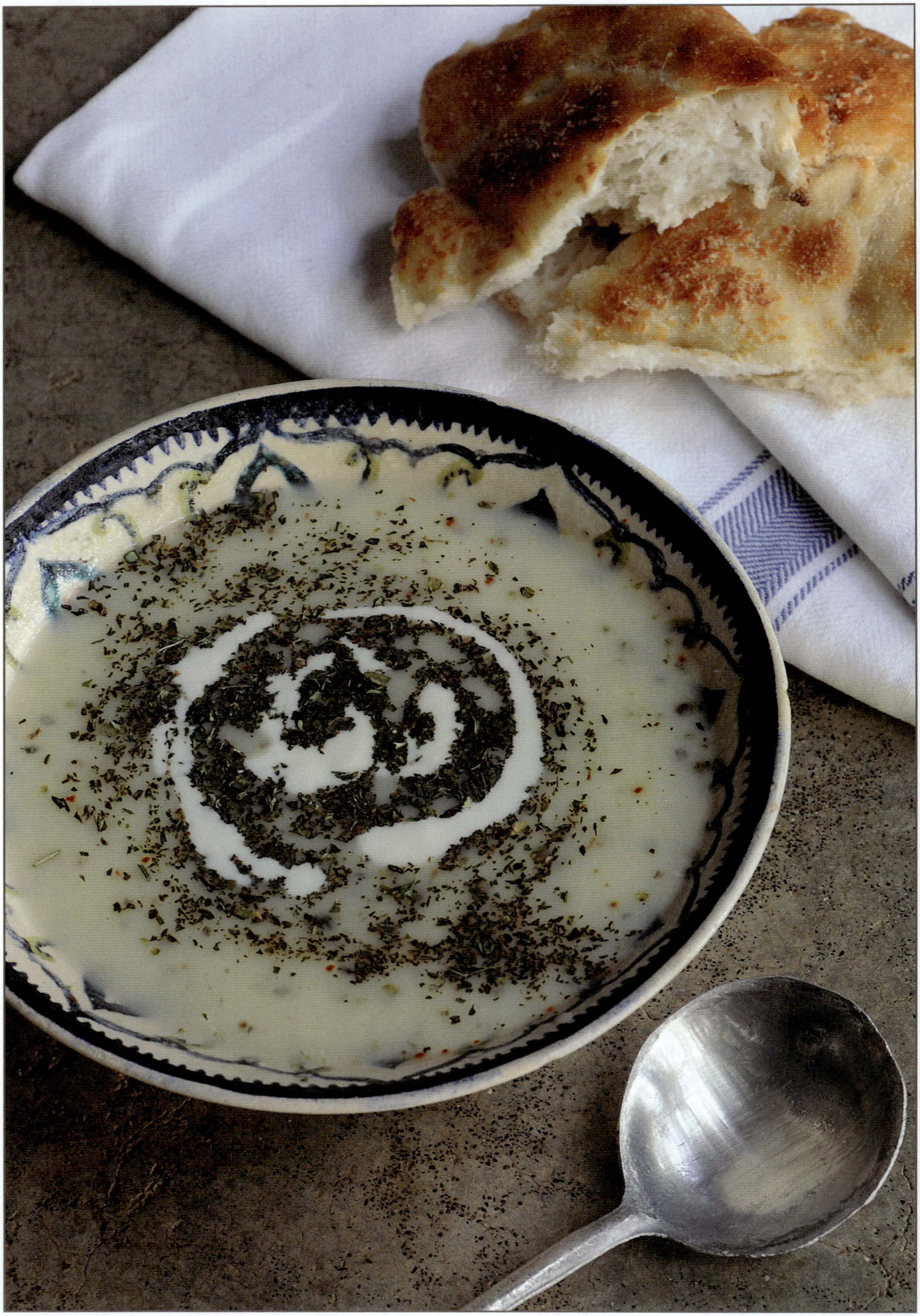

Soups

Soup is a great favourite in Turkey, so much so that there are restaurants that specialise in it and sell nothing else. Sometimes they specialise in just one type of soup. It is consumed at all times of the day, even sometimes for breakfast or in the middle of the night. Lemon juice or vinegar are often used to sharpen the flavours – soup is commonly served with a wedge of lemon. In keeping with this tradition Sevgi makes a wide range of delicious soups.

You can use homemade stock from vegetables or use a bought stock cube. If using a stock cube try using less than half of what the manufacturer recommends as otherwise it can overpower the natural flavours of the soup.

Home made vegetable stock

1 onion
1 carrot
1 potato
1 teaspoon salt
black pepper
1 bay leaf
1.5 litres of water

Before using in the recipe remove and discard the vegetables. (Or eat them as a snack with butter, salt, pepper and grated cheese!)

Patates Çorbası (Potato Soup)

4 potatoes
2 onions
1 teaspoon salt
1 teaspoon dried mint
1 teaspoon dried thyme
25 grms butter
1 tablespoon oil
1 grated tomato
1 litre vegetable stock
2 cups milk
parsley to garnish

Peel and slice the potatoes and onions. Add the butter and oil to a pan and fry the onions and potatoes gently until softened. Add the grated tomato and fry for a minute or two. Add the salt, thyme, mint, stock and milk and bring to the boil. Simmer for 20 minutes until the potatoes are soft, then blend. Serve with a swirl of yogurt and a sprinkle of mint.

Yayla Çorbası (Summer pasture or yogurt soup)

2 onions
50 grms rice
1 litre stock
1 cup yogurt
1 dessert spoon dried mint
salt
2 tablespoons butter or olive oil

This is one of the most distinctive and delicious Turkish soups – and my favourite. Chop the onions finely and fry in the butter until soft. Wash and drain the rice and add to the onions. Stir for a few moments. Add the stock, and salt bring to the boil and simmer for 20 minutes, or until rice is very soft. Stir in the yogurt and mint, and serve with a wedge of lemon.

Ezogelin Çorbası (Bride's Soup)

100 grms red lentils
2 tablespoons butter or olive oil
2 onions
2 green peppers
1 tablespoon tomato puree
1 cup plain yogurt
1 bulb garlic
1 litre stock
half teaspoon pul biber (red pepper flakes) or chilli powder
teaspoon thyme
teaspoon mint
1 bay leaf
salt

Fry the finely chopped onions and peppers, with pepper flakes or chilli powder. When softened add the lentils and fry for a few moments. Add the stock, bring to the boil and simmer for twenty minutes. Smash the garlic in a pestle and mortar, or with the end of a rolling pin, and add to the soup with the salt. In a small bowl blend the tomato puree with the yogurt and herbs, then add the paste to the soup. Simmer for a further three minutes and serve with a sprinkle of parsley.

Yaz – Kış Çorbası (Summer – Winter Soup)

half cup cannellini beans (dry) or 400 grm tin
half cup chick peas (dry) or 400 grm tin
half cup split peas soaked
1 onion
1 tablespoon butter
1 tablespoon olive oil
3 cups yogurt
1 dessert spoon dried mint
salt
1 teaspoon red pepper flakes
1 litre stock

If using dried beans, soak overnight. Cook the beans and split peas in fresh water until they are soft, adding more water if necessary. Fry the finely chopped onion in the olive oil, and then add the cooked beans in their stock, with the salt, and cook for another 15 minutes. Add the yogurt and mint and simmer for a few more minutes. Melt the butter in a small pan and add a teaspoon of red pepper flakes or a generous pinch of chilli and a pinch of paprika and fry gently for a moment. Pour the hot butter mixture, as a garnish onto the soup before serving.

Mercimek Çorbası (Turkish lentil soup)

100 grms red lentils
2 onions
2 tablespoons oil
1 litre stock
1 bay leaf
salt

The trick with Turkish lentil soup is to grate, or better still, finely chop the onions in a food processor. They need to be reduced to a fine pulp. Fry this gently in the oil until soft, and then add the lentils and stock. Bring to the boil and then simmer until the lentils are soft before adding the salt. The soup can then be sieved or blended to a smooth consistency. Serve with a sprinkle of parsley and a wedge of lemon.

Un Çorbası (Flour Soup)

1 litre stock
4 tablespoons butter
4 tablespoons flour
salt
red pepper flakes
4 slices bread
olive oil
lemon

This is one of the simplest soups there is. Warming and filling, from the most simple ingredients, a soup eaten in hard times! Melt the butter and add the flour and lightly brown it. Slowly add the stock, stirring continuously, cover and simmer for 15 minutes, stirring occasionally. Melt a tablespoon of butter and add the red pepper flakes. Drizzle over the soup and serve with a squeeze of lemon juice.

Pirinçli Çorbası (Rice Soup)

50 grms rice
2 onions
1 lemon
2 tablespoons olive oil
1 teaspoon red pepper flakes
or half teaspoon each or chilli and paprika
1 litre stock
salt

Finely chop the onion and fry gently in the oil. Add the red pepper flakes and fry for another minute. Wash and drain the rice, and add. Add the stock, bring to the boil and simmer until rice is very soft and has added its starch to the soup. Add lemon and salt to taste and serve with a sprinkle of red pepper and a small knob of butter as garnish.

Domates Çorbası (Tomato Soup)

1 kilo ripe tomatoes or two tins chopped tomatoes
2 onions
2 tablespoons olive oil
1 clove garlic
1 litre stock
1 teaspoon lemon juice
bay leaf
salt and pepper
2 tablespoons finely grated cheese (cheddar type)
1 cup of cream
basil to garnish

If using fresh tomatoes plunge into boiling water to remove the skins. Finely chop the tomatoes and onions. Crush the garlic. Fry gently in the olive oil until soft. Add the stock, salt, pepper, bay leaf and lemon juice. Simmer gently until all the ingredients blend. Remove the bay leaf and whizz with a blender. Add the grated cheese, and just before serving slowly add the cream while stirring to avoid curdling. Serve with a swirl of cream and a pinch of shredded fresh basil.

Kabak Çorbası (Courgette Soup)

5 courgettes
2 onions
1 tablespoon butter
1 cup yogurt
sprigs of dill
1 cup of peas
1 litre stock
salt
black pepper

Finely dice the courgettes and the onions and gently fry in the butter until transparent. Add the peas if uncooked, and the stock, and simmer gently until the ingredients are soft. If using frozen or tinned peas add them only a minute or two before serving. Add the yogurt and dill, and salt and pepper to taste. Serve with dill garnish.

Düğün Çorbası (Wedding Soup with sour sauce)

2 onions
2 carrots
salt
4 tablespoons butter
2 tablespoons flour
3 egg yolks
juice of 1 lemon
1 tsp red pepper flakes
1 ½ litre water

Terbiye (Sour sauce)

A distinctive addition to many Turkish soups is terbiye, a tart sauce made with egg yolk and lemon juice, which also thickens the soup. Sometimes cream is also added.

Make stock with the water, peeled whole onions, carrots and salt. Simmer until tender, adding more water if necessary. Remove the vegetables and set aside. Melt the butter in a pan, add the flour and brown lightly for 2-3 minutes. Slowly add some stock stirring continuously, until sufficiently thin to add to the soup pan.

Put 3 egg yolks in a bowl and add the lemon juice and beat well, while adding a little stock. Add this mixture to the soup and remove from the heat. Melt a tablespoon of butter in a pan with the red pepper flakes and pour onto the soup before serving.

Mantar Çorbası (Mushroom Soup)

1 kilo mushrooms
2 tablespoons butter
1 clove garlic
1 litre milk
salt
black pepper

For this recipe use mushrooms which have 'gone over' – a bit black and soft. Finely chop the mushrooms and crush the garlic. Gently fry them in the butter, cover with a lid and cook gently until they have 'sweated' out mushroom liquor and are very soft. Add the milk, salt and pepper to taste and simmer until all the ingredients are soft and blended. Whizz with a hand-held blender to a smooth consistency. For a more intense taste, you might like to add a mushroom stock cube. Garnish with flakes of Turkish red pepper, or a sprinkle of paprika.

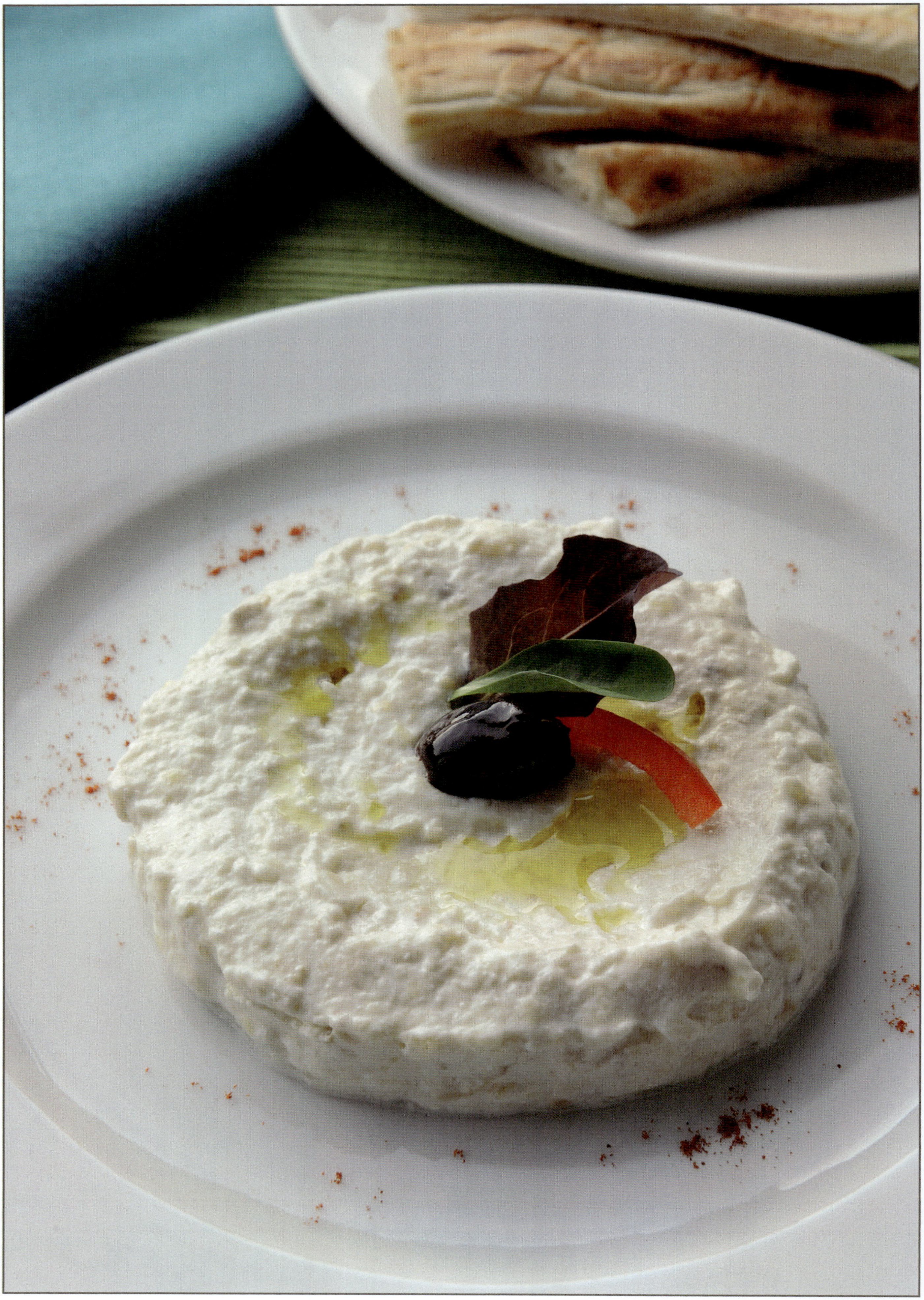

SALADS and APPETIZERS

Vegetables are an important part of the Turkish diet, and freshly prepared salads are served with nearly all meals. Tomatoes, cucumbers and olives are even served as part of a traditional Turkish breakfast. Salads and appetizers range from simple combinations of leafy greens with tomatoes, cucumbers and peppers, to a wide variety made with cooked vegetables, pulses, grains and gallons of olive oil!

One of Turkish cuisine's great features is meze. Literally meaning 'table', the endless variety of small plates of vegetable, pulse and rice appetizers can make up a meal in itself. Vegetables are stuffed with rice, currants, and pine nuts; seasonal vegetables are cooked in olive oil and served with yogurt garlic sauce; and the ubiquitous aubergine is prepared as a puree, or stuffed with tomatoes, onions, garlic and parsley to create the famous Imam Bayildi which translates as 'the Imam fainted' – the implication being that he fainted with pleasure! A second version of this tale is that he fainted at the cost of the olive oil used in the recipe.

Many of the recipes in this section can be eaten as a starter if served in traditional small portions, or as part of a main meal. Traditionally they are often served cold, but are equally delicious served warm.

Yoğurtlu Patlıcan Salatası (Grilled Aubergine Salad with Yogurt)

4 large aubergines
4 tablespoons lemon juice
4 tablespoons olive oil
1 teaspoon salt
4 cloves garlic
4 tablespoons yogurt
a few black olives
parsley
red pepper flakes or paprika

Place the oil and lemon juice in a bowl. Prepare the aubergines by placing them whole in their skins under a medium grill until they are burnt on the outside and very soft on the inside, turning when necessary. Hold each aubergine by the stem and hold under cold running water for a few seconds. The skin should then peel off. Remove the stem and place the aubergines one at a time into the lemon and oil mixture, mashing them with a fork until the mixture is smooth. Add the crushed garlic, salt and yogurt, mixing well. Arrange on a serving dish. Garnish with a drizzle of olive oil, a sprinkle of red pepper flakes, a sprig of parsley and the olives. Serve with crusty bread.

Yoğurtlu Havuç Salatası (Carrot yogurt salad with tahini and walnuts)

5 medium carrots
3 tablespoons olive oil
3 tablespoons yogurt
3 tablespoons tahini
3 tablespoons chopped walnuts
2- 4 cloves garlic
salt
1 tsp red pepper flakes or paprika
knob of butter

Grate the carrots and sauté in the olive oil with some salt. Crush the garlic and add to the yogurt. Mix the yogurt, tahini, walnuts, half the red pepper and salt with the carrots. Turn into a serving dish. Melt a knob of butter in a pan and stir in the remaining red pepper flakes or paprika so the butter turns red. Drizzle over salad. Serve with crusty bread.

Çoban Salatası (Shepherd's Salad)

4 large tomatoes
1 mild onion
2 green peppers
1 cucumber
large bunch of flat leaf parsley
a handful black olives
2 tablespoons olive oil
2 tablespoons lemon juice
½ tsp salt

This is a very simple but delicious salad. The trick is to apply the dressing 10 minutes before serving as it draws out the juices from the ingredients. The test of a good shepherd's salad is that the juice left in the dish is good enough to drink – or to dip a chunk of bread in.

Peel, seed and coarsely chop the tomatoes. Remove the pepper seeds and slice finely. Peel and dice the cucumber. Coarsely chop the parsley. Mix the ingredients and sprinkle with salt. Drizzle with the olive oil, and lemon juice. Garnish with the olives.
You can also add 100 grms of diced feta cheese to this recipe if you wish.

Kırımızı Laharna Salatası (Red cabbage salad)

1 small red cabbage or ½ medium one
1 bunch flat leaf parsley
1 teaspoon salt
2 tablespoons of lemon juice
2 tablespoons olive oil
2 tablespoons red wine vinegar

Finely shred the cabbage and mix with the vinegar and salt. Cover and leave in the fridge for a few hours or overnight. To serve, drain any liquor from the cabbage, and then mix with the chopped parsley, olive oil and lemon juice.

Yoğurtlu Havuç Kızartma (Crispy batter carrots and yogurt)

5 – 6 medium carrots
100 grms flour
1 cup yogurt
½ cup olive oil
salt
1½ cups water

Peel the carrots and cut them lengthwise into flat strips. Simmer in a little water until softened. Drain and cool. Add a pinch of salt to the flour and slowly add the water stirring constantly until the mixture is smooth and creamy. Heat the olive oil in a frying pan. Dip the carrot slices into the batter mix and fry on each side until they are golden brown. Serve with salted yogurt.

Semizotu Salatası (Purslane salad with garlic and lemon)

Purslane resembles a fleshier version of watercress and has a fresh lemony flavour. You can find it in some supermarkets.

1 bunch purslane
2 thinly sliced garlic cloves
1 thinly sliced carrot
2 tablespoons olive oil
2 tablespoons wine vinegar
½ teaspoon mustard
salt
pepper
lemon juice

Wash and drain the purslane. Use the smaller leaves and stems whole, chop any larger stems. Slice the garlic very thinly and leave in lemon juice for 30 minutes. Finely slice or grate the carrot. Combine the ingredients, and pour over the olive oil, vinegar, salt, pepper and mustard dressing.

Tost Salatası (Toast Salad)

1 loaf bread
½ bunch spring onions
½ bunch fresh mint
½ bunch purslane
1 bunch flat leaf parsley
1 small lettuce
4 tomatoes
2 garlic cloves
3 tablespoons lemon juice
3 tablespoons olive oil
salt
freshly ground black pepper

Finely slice the garlic and leave on one side in lemon juice for 30 minutes.
Remove the crusts from the loaf and cut the bread into small cubes. Toast them in a dry frying pan until golden brown, or alternatively on a tray in a hot oven. Chop the parsley, mint and spring onions. Peel and slice the tomatoes and cucumber into rings.
Shred the lettuce and purslane. Combine all the ingredients and dress with lemon juice, oil, salt and black pepper. Toss before serving. Garnish with a few sprigs of mint.

Sigara Börek

Humus

Sigara Börek ('Cigarette' feta cheese and herb filo parcels)

These crispy 'cigarette' shaped parcels of filo pastry and herb cheese are a classic Turkish meze.

I would recommend buying filo pastry rather than struggling to make great sheets of wafer thin pastry, which is quite an art! It is available in Turkish shops, known as 'yufka' or is now available as filo from the freezer cabinet of most supermarkets. Yufka comes ready rolled in large circles. Filo will have to be rolled or cut into an 18 inch diameter.

- **3 circular sheets of yufka or filo pastry**
- **200 – 300 grms feta cheese**
- **1 egg**
- **½ bunch parsley finely chopped**
- **½ bunch dill**
- **teaspoon red pepper flakes (optional for a spicier taste)**
- **olive or sunflower oil for frying**

Mash the cheese, beat and add the egg and finely chopped herbs and combine together. Place the 3 circular sheets of filo on top of each other. Fold in half and cut along the fold to create two semicircles. Place on top of each other. Cut the semicircles into 4 triangular shaped pieces, making 24 equal sized triangles of filo. Place a teaspoon of the cheese mix on to the middle of the wide end of the triangle. Fold in the ends and roll into a cigarette shape, with a dab of water wet the end to seal it. Heat the oil and deep fry the borek over a medium heat until golden brown. Drain on kitchen towel and serve hot.

Domates Salatası (Tomato and basil salad)

This simple salad is easy and delicious.

- **6 Tomatoes**
- **fresh basil leaves or dessertspoon dried basil**
- **Juice of one lemon**
- **olive oil**
- **salt**
- **freshly ground black pepper**

Slice the tomatoes and arrange on a plate or shallow serving dish. (I always find this looks twice as delicious when served on a blue plate!) Squeeze over the lemon, drizzle with oil and sprinkle with salt, shredded basil and ground pepper. Leave for 10 minutes before serving which allows the flavours to absorb each other. You are also then left with a liquor which the salt draws out and which begs to be mopped up with a piece of crusty bread!

Patlıcan Kızartma (Fried Aubergine Fritters with Yogurt)

2 medium aubergines
2 tablespoons flour
½ level teaspoon baking powder
300 mls milk and water (or milk and beer)
1 egg
salt
olive oil for frying

Wash the aubergines and remove the stalk. Slice at an angle into long ovals about ¼ inch thick. Place in a bowl of cold salted water for 20 minutes, rinse, drain and pat dry. Make a batter by sifting the flour and baking powder together in a mixing bowl, add the egg and blend slowly with the milk/water mixture until the consistency of smooth cream. Add a small pinch of salt. Heat oil in a frying pan until a drop of mixture sizzles gently. Dip the aubergine slices in the batter and fry gently on both sides until golden – about two or three mintutes each side. The aubergine should be very soft, and the batter crumbly. Serve with plain or garlic yogurt drizzled with a little olive oil. Or gently fry some red pepper flakes in butter and pour over before serving.

Mucver (Courgette, Feta and Dill Fritters)

2 large or 4 small courgettes
50 grms crumbled feta cheese
2 tablespoons flour
½ level teaspoon baking powder
300 mls milk and water (you can substitute beer for water for extra lightness)
1 egg
olive oil for frying
salt
pepper
fresh or dried dill

Wash and coarsely grate the courgettes. Sift the flour and baking powder together into a mixing bowl. Break the egg into the flour and with a little of the milk and water mix gradually blend to the consistency of cream. Stir in the grated courgettes and crumbled feta, and some of the dill chopped. Reserve some dill to garnish. Heat the olive oil in a frying pan until a test droplet sizzles gently. Add the mixture in tablespoon size dollops to form little flat fritters and fry gently on both sides until golden. Lovely served with garlic salted yogurt.

Humus (Chickpea, Sesame, Garlic and Lemon Dip)

2 tins of cooked chickpeas (reserve the water)
juice of 2 lemons
2 tblsp olive oil
4 – 6 cloves garlic
1 tsp salt
6 tblsps tahini (sesame paste)

Blend all the ingredients in a food processor, or mash thoroughly. If the mixture is too thick add a little of the reserved chickpea water or a little more olive oil. Adjust the lemon, salt and garlic ratio to taste. Serve garnished with red pepper flakes and drizzle with olive oil.

Imam Bayıldı

Imam Bayıldı
(The Imam Fainted – aubergine stuffed with tomatoes & peppers with olive oil)

4 aubergines
2 cups olive oil
2 onions
4 cloves garlic
8 tomatoes
1 bunch parsley
2 green peppers
1 teaspoon sugar
salt and freshly ground pepper

This dish calls for the aubergines to be peeled in alternate lengthways strips – to give a striped effect. This helps the cooking process while holding the aubergine together. Make a slit to form a 'pocket' in the aubergine. Sprinkle generously with salt, cover with cold water, and set aside for 20 minutes. (I sometimes dispense with this traditional procedure when I'm in a hurry, and I haven't noticed much difference – but you may prefer to do it by the book)

Finely chop the onions, garlic, tomatoes and parsley and add to gently warming olive oil in a frying pan. Season with salt and pepper and add the sugar. Fry gently for a few moments, before adding a few tablespoons of water, cover the pan and simmer for 10 minutes, or until the onions are soft.

Rinse the aubergines in cold water and pat dry with kitchen towel. Fry the aubergines, turning in an inch or two of olive oil until they are lightly browned on all sides. Remove with a slotted spoon and place in a baking dish open side up. Add the sliced green peppers to the pan and fry for a couple of minutes. (if you can acquire the long pepper variety, then split them lengthways, otherwise cut a bell pepper into rings).
Fill the split aubergines with the tomato mixture, and lay a halved green pepper, or a few rings, on top. Drizzle the remaining olive oil over them, and add half a cup of water to the dish. Bake for 30 minutes in a moderate oven. Can be served hot or cold. This dish, although traditionally a starter, also makes a delicious main course served with rice and yogurt.

Roka Sarmasaklı Salatası (Rocket, garlic, feta and sesame seed salad)

1 bunch rocket
1 small lettuce
150 grms feta cheese
6 cloves garlic sliced
3 tablespoons wine vinegar
4 tablespoons olive oil
1- 2 tablespoons sesame seeds
salt

Toast the sesame seeds over a medium heat in a dry frying pan until golden. Set aside. Saute the garlic slices in a tablespoon of the olive oil until golden brown. Remove and set aside. Add the sesame seeds, vinegar, and salt and cook over a low heat for a few minutes before adding the remaining olive oil. Remove from the heat. Shred the lettuce and add the rocket, arranging in a bowl. Crumble the cheese over the top, add the dressing and finally scatter the golden garlic slices on top.

Karnibahar Salatası (Cauliflower, sesame and lemon salad)

1 small cauliflower
1 cup of milk
juice of 2 lemons
2 cloves garlic
2 tablespoons tahini
salt
red pepper flakes or paprika
olive oil
parsley

Divide the cauliflower into florets, simmer in milk with salt until tender but firm. Drain and place in serving dish. Blend the tahini, lemon juice, crushed garlic, pinch of salt, red pepper and some of the milk to create a creamy thick sauce. Add a little more tahini if necessary. Pour the sauce onto the warm cauliflower and allow to cool and absorb the flavours. Drizzle with olive oil and garnish with chopped parsley and red pepper flakes.

Pilaki (Butter Bean and Red Onion Salad)

400 grms cooked butter beans
1 red onion
clove garlic crushed (optional)
bunch flat leaf parsley
2-3 tablespoons lemon juice
1 tablespoon olive oil
salt
¼ teaspoon red pepper flakes

Drain a can of butter beans (or cook your own). This recipe works best if the beans are warm when adding the oil and lemon mix. Finely slice the onion and sprinkle with salt. Set aside for 10 minutes. Add the oil, lemon juice, garlic and seasoning to taste to the warm beans. Allow to cool, then combine with the onions and shredded parsley. Sprinkle with pepper flakes. Serve with a green salad and crusty bread.

Bezelye Salatası (Pea, apple and mint salad)

250 grms cooked peas
1 apple
1 carrot
1 dessertspoon lemon juice
1 dessertspoon fresh chopped mint or 1 teaspoon of dried mint
1 dessertspoon olive oil
pinch sugar
¼ - ½ teaspoon salt

Grate the apple and mix with the lemon juice to prevent browning. Grate the carrot and chop the mint. Mix the grated apple, carrot, parsley and cooked peas together. Add the oil, salt and mint.

Rumelia Salatası (Potato Salad with boiled eggs and black olives)

4 medium potatoes
2 hardboiled eggs
2 small red onions
bunch parsley
3 tablespoons olive oil
3 tablespoons lemon juice
¼ - ½ tsp salt
black pepper
black olives to garnish
100 grms chicken livers (optional)

Peel and cut potatoes into small cubes. Boil gently in salted water until soft but firm. Drain and set aside. Whisk the oil and lemon together with the salt and pour over the warm potatoes. Finely slice the onions into half moons, and coarsely chop the parsley, and add to the potatoes. If using liver, chop finely and fry gently until it changes colour, but remains soft. Turn out potato mix onto a dish and garnish with slices of egg, parsley, black olives and coarsely ground black pepper

Cacık (Garlic Cucumber Yogurt)

500 grms yogurt
1 cucumber
1 level teaspoon salt
1 clove of crushed garlic (or more if you love garlic)
2 tablespoons olive oil
1 teaspoon dried mint
2 sprigs of dill
half cup of water

Peel and chop the cucumbers into tiny pieces. (Some people prefer to leave the peel on – experiment!) Sprinkle the cucumber pieces with salt and set aside. Beat the yogurt well, and slowly add up to a cup of water, until it is the consistency of creamy soup. (Indeed it is a sort of cold soup) Add the salted cucumbers and crushed garlic. Sprinkle with the mint and chopped dill. Garnish with a swirl of olive oil and serve chilled.

Pancar Salatası (Beetroot and Tahini Salad)

6 medium sized beetroot
4 cloves garlic
4 dessert spoons tahini
4 dessert spoons lemon juice
4 dessertspoons olive oil
salt

Roast the unpeeled beetroot in the oven with a little olive oil at 200 C for 45 mins or until soft. When cool, peel and grate, or put in a food processor. Add the tahini, crushed garlic, lemon juice, olive oil, salt to taste and mix. Serve garnished with fennel. This salad has the most sensational colour and is a stunning addition to any meal. Lovely as a dip with strips of warm pitta bread.

Bakla Puresi (Broad Bean Paté)

500 grms shelled broad beans – fresh or frozen
1 clove garlic crushed
1 tablespoons olive oil
1 tablespoon lemon juice
1 tablespoon yogurt
salt
pepper
1 teaspoon dried mint
1 teaspoon red pepper flakes (optional spicy version)

This is a sort of broad bean hummus. Simmer the beans until soft (about 10 mins). Drain, mash and blend with the other ingredients. Garnish with a drizzle of olive oil and a sprinkle of mint or red pepper. Serve with strips of warm pitta bread.

Peynirli Mantar (Cheese Stuffed Mushrooms with crispy breadcrumb topping)

8 large flat mushrooms
100 grms grated cheese
100 grms breadcrumbs
parsley to garnish

Wipe the mushrooms with a clean damp cloth and remove the stalks. Place in an oiled shallow casserole dish. Sprinkle with the cheese and bake for about 15 minutes at 200 C. Preheat the grill. Remove the mushrooms from the oven and sprinkle with the breadcrumbs. Place under a medium grill until breadcrumbs turn golden. Serve with a sprinkle of finely chopped parsley.

Taze Fasulye (Green beans in olive oil and tomato sauce)

500 grms green beans (runner, French or fine)
1 large onion
4 ripe tomatoes
1 clove garlic (optional)
1 tablespoon olive oil
salt

Wash and trim the beans, runner beans can be sliced, French or fine beans can be left whole. Slice the onion in half moons. Remove the tomato skins by plunging into very hot water, after which the skin will come away easily. Finely chop. Add the onions (and crushed garlic if required) to the olive oil and gently fry until soft, add the chopped tomatoes and salt and continue to cook for a few minutes. Add the beans and a little water if necessary to just cover and simmer gently until softened and the tomato sauce is reduced. Can be eaten warm or cold, with crusty bread.

Fasulye Piyazı (Canellini Bean Salad)

- 250 grms dry canellini beans or 2 tins ready cooked
- 4 dessertspoons wine vinegar
- 1 onion
- 3 tomatoes
- 3 peppers
- bunch parsley
- 3 hard boiled eggs
- 2 teaspoons salt
- 3 tablespoons olive oil

If you are using dry beans, soak overnight and then place in fresh water, bring to the boil and cook on a medium heat for about 40 minutes or until soft. (Pressure cookers are great for beans, but you have to be careful not to overdo them or they become squishy.) Drain the beans, and while warm, sprinkle with salt and half the vinegar. Set aside for a couple of hours to allow the beans to absorb the flavours.

Slice the onions lengthways. Sprinkle with salt and leave for ten minutes to extract the volatile juices, before washing and draining. This is an old Turkish trick with onions that makes them very tasty in salads.

Drain any excess vinegar from the beans. Add the onions and chopped parsley and mix well. Turn out onto a serving dish and garnish, with finely sliced peppers, tomatoes and egg Mix the remaining vinegar with the oil and salt and pour over the beans.

Ezme (Spicy tomato, pepper and cucumber dip)

This hot concoction is traditionally from Eastern Turkey where food is generally much spicier.

- 4 large ripe tomatoes
- 2 green peppers
- 1 cucumber
- 2 cloves garlic
- 3 spring onions
- 1 teaspoon dried mint
- ½ - 1 teaspoon red pepper flakes
- or quarter teaspoon each of paprika and chilli
- 1 teaspooon freshly ground black pepper
- 3 tablespoons olive oil
- 2 tablespoons lemon juice
- teaspoon tomato puree
- salt

Peel the tomatoes and cucumber. Remove the seeds and stalk from the pepper. Chop all the ingredients very finely, until they become a textured paste. (Or use a food processor on just two or three pulses) Add the oil, lemon and seasonings, and mix well.

This dish is one of my favourites and makes a lovely lunchtime snack with a green salad and a crusty baguette.

Patlıcan Börek (Deep fried cheese stuffed aubergines)

Fiddly – and fattening - but spectacular and delicious! This recipe calls for quite a lot of olive oil, but is worth it once in a while!

4 small aubergines
400 grms feta cheese
4 eggs
bunch parsley
large cup breadcrumbs
olive oil for deep frying

Peel aubergines lengthwise leaving the skin in alternate stripes, leaving the stalk and end intact. Salt all over and leave aside for half an hour to remove bitter juices. (With modern varieties of aubergine this seems less necessary) Rinse and dry well. Deep fry the aubergines in the oil over a medium heat until they are golden. Remove with slotted spoon onto kitchen paper to drain and cool. The aubergines should be tender but with the stem intact.

Beattwo eggs and combine with mashed feta cheese, add the finely chopped parsley and mix well. Make a slit lengthways in the cooled aubergines to make a pocket for the cheese mix and remove some of the flesh.

Add the cheese mix and close the slits –the cheese shouldn't be visible. Dip in the remaining beaten egg and roll in breadcrumbs and deep fry on a medium heat for 5-6 minutes until the breadcrumbs are golden brown.

Pırasa Cevizli Mucver (Leek and walnut fritters)

3 leeks
100 grms feta cheese
3 eggs
2 tblsp flour
5 tbslp chopped walnuts
black pepper to taste
olive oil

Finely slice the leeks and simmer gently in a little water until softened. Drain. Mash the cheese (don't add salt as the cheese is usually salty) add the crushed walnuts and pepper. Add the beaten eggs to the flour and mix into a batter. Add a little milk if the batter is too stiff. Fold in the leeks and cheese mix.

Add enough olive oil to shallow fry. Over a medium heat drop tablespoons of the mix into the oil and press lightly with the back of a spoon to flatten. Cook each side until golden brown, and drain on kitchen paper. Delicious served with lightly salted yogurt.

Yaprak Dolması (Vine leaves stuffed with cinnamon, pine nut and currant rice)

These little parcels of fragrant rice in vine leaves are a quintessential Mediterranean dish, and surprisingly easy to make. Fresh vine leaves (if you're lucky enough to have them) need to be softened in boiling salted water, or use the preserved variety from Turkish or Greek shops – these can be salty and may need to be rinsed a few times. An alternative is to use cabbage leaves. If using cabbage, slice in half, removing the heart. Simmer for 5 minutes in boiling water until softened, before rinsing in cold water. Separate the layers of leaves, cutting away any veins.

- **20 vine leaves or one medium cabbage**
- **rice stuffing (see page 43)**
- **olive oil**
- **cup hot water**
- **juice of 1 lemon**
- **lemon wedges**
- **salt**
- **1 teaspoon sugar**
- **fresh dill to garnish**

Place a heaped teaspoon of rice mix at the base of the leaf, folding the edges in and rolling into a finger shape. Arrange the 'dolma' (stuffed) seam down in a large pan, packed in rows and layers to keep them in place. Mix the water with the lemon juice, olive oil, sugar and salt and pour over. Place a plate over the dolma to fit inside the pan. Cover and cook on a low heat for about 25 minutes. Allow to cool before arranging on a serving dish with a drizzle of olive oil, lemon wedges and sprigs of dill.

Yoğurtlu Semizotu (Purslane and garlic yogurt with pepper butter sauce)

- **1 bunch purslane (or watercress)**
- **2 cups yogurt**
- **1-2 crushed garlic cloves**
- **salt**
- **1 tablespoon butter**
- **½ teaspoon red pepper**

Wash, drain and chop the purslane. Combine the yogurt with the salt and crushed garlic and mix with the purslane. Melt the butter and gently fry the red pepper flakes, or paprika, for a minute. Drizzle over the yogurt and purslane.

Yaprak Dolması

Kısır

MAIN DISHES

A Turkish speciality are vegetables stuffed with lovely aromatic rice mixes, so the recipes in this section are for a variety of pilavs and bulgurs, which can be used to accompany main dishes, or to create the various vegetable dolma (literally meaning 'stuffed').

Originating from China, rice was introduced to Turkey through Persian dishes and is now a staple of the Turkish diet although for many years it was mainly a rich man's dish. In the villages, bulgur (crushed wheat) is still generally used instead of rice. The following dishes can also be made using the bulgur recipes as stuffing.

Cevizli Kısır (Bulgur with crushed walnuts and fresh herbs)

- 2 cups bulgur
- 2 cups boiling water
- 1 tablespoon olive oil
- 1 tablespoon butter
- 4 tomatoes skinned and finely chopped
- 1 cup crushed walnuts
- handful fresh chopped mint
- handful fresh chopped parsley
- 4 or 5 spring onions finely sliced
- ½ teaspoon salt

Prepare the bulgur by adding the boiling water and leaving over a very low heat until all the water is absorbed and the bulgur is soft. Add more hot water if necessary.
Gently fry the peeled, chopped tomatoes in the olive oil and butter until soft. Add to the warm bulgur with the walnuts, chopped mint, parsley and sliced spring onions. Add salt to taste.

Kısır (Spicy tomato bulgur with parsley and currants)

This recipe is a highly coloured and spicy version of bulgur. I find you can't have too much parsley in this dish, the bright green contrasting with the red spicy bulgur and black currants.

- 2 cups bulgur
- 2 cups boiling water
- 1 - 2 tsp red pepper flakes
- 2 large onions
- 2 tablespoons currants
- 1 – 2 tablespoons tomato puree
- salt
- bunch flat leafed parsley
- 1 tablespoon olive oil
- 1 tablespoon butter

Add boiling water to the bulgur and currants. Leave on a very low heat until all the water is absorbed and bulgur is soft. Add more hot water if necessary. Finely chop the onions and fry in the oil and butter with the red pepper flakes. When the bulgur has absorbed all the water and is soft, add to the onion and pepper mix. Stir in the tomato puree, and chopped parsley. Salt to taste. Serve as an accompaniment to a meal or with a green salad.

Sebzeli Bulgur Pilav (Bulgur pilav with vegetables)

1 cup bulgur
2 cups hot stock
2 cloves garlic
2 large onions
a handful of green beans
1 leek
2 green peppers
2 red peppers
celery
2 carrots
4 tomatoes finely chopped or grated
1 tin chickpeas
1 bunch dill
1 bunch parsley
olive oil
salt, pepper

Pour the stock over the bulgur and simmer over a very gentle heat until all the stock is absorbed, or the bulgur is soft. Finely slice the vegetables and gently fry in olive oil until tender, adding the peppers last so as not to lose their shape and colour. In another pan sauté the drained chickpeas in the olive oil, the grated tomatoes and salt until all the juices are absorbed. Combine the bulgur and warm vegetables. Garnish with a spoonful of the chickpeas, chopped herbs, freshly ground black pepper or red pepper flakes and serve.

Patlıcan Pilav (Aubergine pilav)

2 aubergines
2 tomatoes skinned
250 grms long grain or basmati rice
2 onions
1 tablespoons currants
1 tablespoons pine nuts
1 tablespoon olive oil
1 tablespoon butter
bunch parsley
½ teaspoon cinnamon
½ teaspoon allspice
1 teaspoon black pepper
1 dessertspoon dried mint
½ teaspoon salt
hot water or stock

Cover the rice with plenty of hot salted water and put on one side for 20 minutes. Peel the aubergine in alternate stripes and soak in salt water for 20 minutes. Finely chop the onions and fry gently with the pine nuts in butter and oil until golden. Drain and rinse the softened rice. Add to the onions, pine nuts and butter and gently fry the rice for a few minutes. Add the currants, herbs, spices, salt, pepper and finely chopped tomatoes. Add enough hot stock to cover the rice mix. I always find bought stock/ bouillon rather overpowering for these delicate dishes, so I use it well diluted. Cover with a tight lid and simmer very gently until the rice is soft. Don't stir the rice.
Add a little more hot water if necessary. Take off the heat and leave to stand for a further 10 – 20 minutes. Rinse and pat dry the aubergines, and cut into small cubes. Saute in a little olive oil until browned and soft, remove and drain on kitchen towel. Add the aubergine and freshly chopped parsley to the rice and mix through with a fork. Serve hot, or cold as a salad.

Limonlu Pilav (Lemon Rice)

250 grms basmati or long grain rice
1 lemon
2 tablespoons butter
salt
ground black pepper
1 bunch dill

Cover the rice with boiling water and put aside for 20 minutes. Peel the rind from the lemon, and cut into thin julienne strips. Keep a pan of water simmering and have a bowl of cold water to hand. Dip the rinds into the simmering water for 2 minutes, then remove with a slotted spoon and leave in the cold water for a minute or two. Repeat this process 4 or 5 times to remove the bitterness from the rind. Drain and rinse the rice. Heat the butter in a heavy bottomed pan and add the well drained rice, gently stirring for 2 minutes. Add the lemon rinds and cook for another two minutes. Add hot water and salt to cover the rice. Simmer until water is absorbed and the rice soft. Add more hot water if necessary and continue to steam the rice. Remove from the heat and leave to rest for 10 minutes. Add freshly ground black pepper and chopped dill. Alternatively add a tablespoon of currants when adding the water and garnish with sprinkled cinnamon.

Istanbul Pilav

250 grms of 1 cup of long grained rice
1 tablespoon blanched almonds
1 tablespoon pistachio nuts
½ cup cooked peas
stock
¼ tsp saffron or turmeric
1 tablespoon butter
1 tablespoon olive oil
salt
pepper

Pour boiling water onto the rice, stir and leave to stand for 20 minutes. Soak the nuts in hot water until they swell and it is easy to rub off the skins. Rinse and drain the rice, and nuts. Gently fry the butter and oil, adding the almonds, pistachios and stir for a few minutes before adding the rice. Gently fry for a few more minutes before adding the stock, peas and saffron (or turmeric), salt and pepper. Simmer gently until all the stock is absorbed.

Dolma Içi (Aromatic herbed spiced rice with currants for stuffing vegetables)

250 grms long grain or basmati rice (1 cup)
4 onions
2 tablespoons currants
2 tablespoons pine nuts
1 tablespoon olive oil
1 tablespoon butter
bunch parsley
½ teaspoon cinnamon
½ teaspoon allspice
1 teaspoon black pepper
1 dessertspoon dried mint
dessert spoon tomato puree (optional if you want to colour the rice)
½ teaspoon salt
hot water or stock

Cover the rice with plenty of hot salted water and put on one side for 20 minutes. Finely chop the onions and fry gently with the pine nuts in butter and oil until golden. Drain and rinse the softened rice. Add to the onions, pine nuts and butter and gently fry the rice for a few minutes. Add the currants, herbs, spices, salt and pepper. Add enough hot stock to cover the rice mix. I always find bought stock/ bouillon rather overpowering for these delicate dishes, so I use it well diluted. Cover with a tight lid and simmer very gently until the rice is soft. Don't stir the rice. Add a little more hot water if necessary. Take off the heat and leave to stand for a further 10 – 20 minutes.

Izmir Pilav

Add a few finely cut dried apricots, 2 tablespoons of chopped walnuts or blanched almonds to the above mix, adding with the spices and currants.

Domates Dolması (Rice stuffed tomatoes)

8 large tomatoes
rice stuffing mix (see page 43)
1 cup hot water
2 tablespoons olive oil
½ teaspoon salt
½ teaspoon sugar

Slice the tops from the tomatoes to form little lids. Remove the flesh from inside and finely chop. Place the chopped tomato flesh in the bottom of a greased ovenproof dish. Add the salt, sugar and water and stir. Stuff the tomato shells with the rice mixture, and replace the lids. Pack into the ovenproof dish, on top of the chopped tomato mix, making sure the dolmas remain upright. Drizzle with olive oil. Cover with lid, baking parchment, or foil and bake in a medium oven for 20 - 30 minutes or until tender. Add more water if necessary during cooking.

Biber Dolması (Stuffed bell peppers)

8 large green bell peppers
rice stuffing mix (see page 43)
1 cup hot water
2 tablespoons olive oil
4 skinned and chopped tomatoes
½ teaspoon salt
½ teaspoon sugar

Slice the tops from the peppers to form little lids. Remove pith and seeds from inside the peppers. Finely chop the skinned tomatoes and place in the bottom of a greased ovenproof dish. Add the salt, sugar and water and stir. Stuff the peppers with the rice mixture, and replace the lids or alternatively place a slice of tomato as a lid. Pack into the ovenproof dish, on top of the tomato mix, making sure the peppers remain upright. Drizzle the olive oil over the peppers. Cover with lid, baking parchment, or foil and bake in a medium oven for 30 - 40 minutes or until tender. Add more water if necessary during cooking.

Mercimek Köftesi (Lentil rissoles)

- 2 cups red lentils
- 2 onions
- 1 bunch Italian Parsley
- 3 long green peppers
- 1 tablespoon tomato puree
- 1 teaspoon freshly ground black pepper
- 1 teaspoon cumin
- 2 eggs
- 1 teaspoon salt
- 50 grms flour
- half a cup oil (olive or sunflower)
- water

Slice the onions and peppers very finely, and fry gently until softened. Add the lentils, and stir for a further two minutes. Add the water, bring to the boil and cook for 20 minutes. When all the water has been absorbed by the lentils and they are soft, add the eggs, flour, pepper, salt, tomato puree, cumin and chopped parsley to the mix. Take a dessertspoon of mix and shape into oval flattened rissoles. Use a little flour if necessary to dust your hands. Heat oil in a frying pan. Fry the rissoles on a medium heat until golden brown. Delicious with garlic yogurt.

Kuru Fasulye Piyazı (Bean Pilaki with Tarator Sauce)

- 2 tins haricot beans
- 2 onions
- 4 cloves garlic
- 2 tomatoes (skinned)
- 3 – 4 green peppers (long variety)
- 4 tablespoons olive oil
- ½ - 1 tsp salt
- ½ - 1 tsp sugar

Tarator Sauce

This is one of the classic sauces of Turkey made with walnuts, garlic and bread.

- 1 cup shelled walnuts
- 4 slices stale bread
- 2 tablespoons olive oil
- 1 tablespoon white wine vinegar
- 2 tablespoons lemon juice
- 4 cloves garlic
- 2 tablespoons milk

Slice the onions and peel the cloves of garlic, leaving them whole. Sauté in the oil for a few minutes. Stir in the skinned, chopped tomatoes and cook until tender. Add the cooked beans with the sugar and salt. Place the peppers on top and simmer gently until the liquid is reduced to a sauce. Leave to cool.

To make the tarator sauce, crush the walnuts in a mortar. Soak the bread in water, before squeezing it dry and then mix it with the walnuts and the olive oil. Crush the garlic cloves, adding the salt, vinegar and lemon juice. Beat in the milk little by little until the mixture is creamy. Blend the bread walnut mix with the garlic lemon milk cream. Arrange the pilaki on a plate and pour over the tarator sauce before serving. Garnish with parsley.

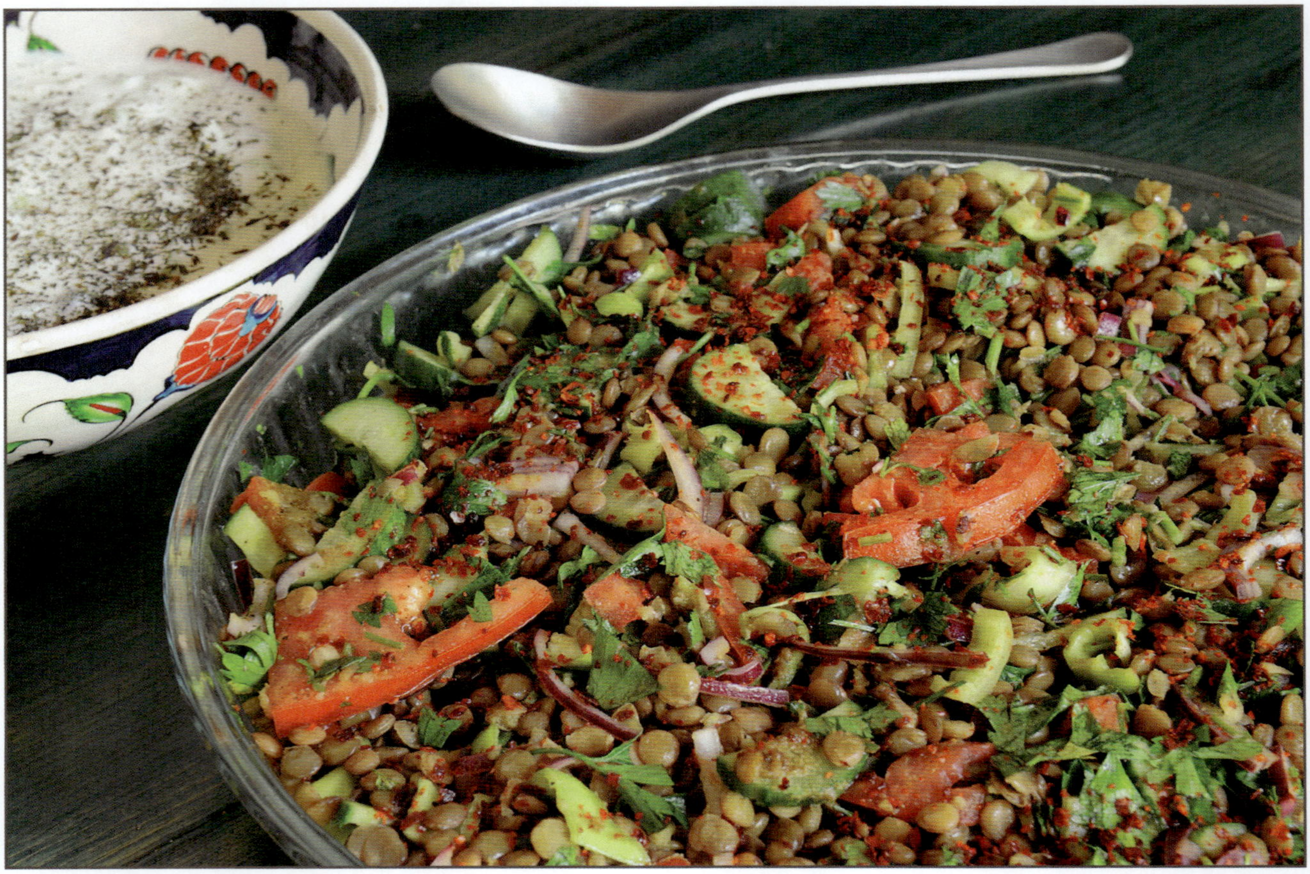

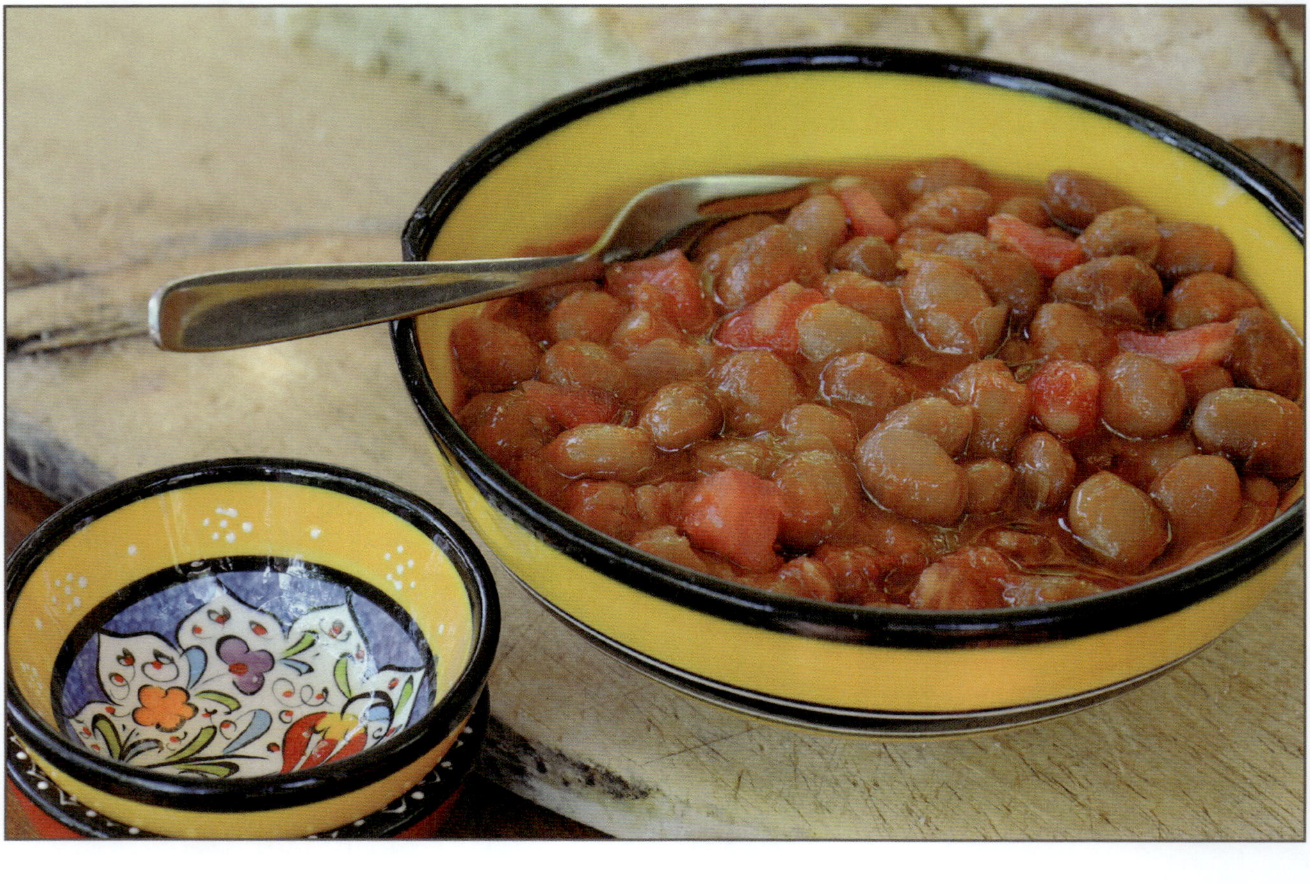

Yesil Mercimek (Green lentils with lemon dressing)

Green lentils are very nutritious and this makes a sustaining side dish served warm, or cold as a salad.

200 grms green lentils (1 cup)
2 onions
2 carrots
2 cloves garlic
2 tomatoes
4 tablespoons lemon juice
3 tablespoons olive oil (2 for dressing)
2 hard boiled eggs for garnish
hot water
½ tsp salt
pinch sugar
red pepper
bunch parsley

Cover the lentils with hot water and leave for an hour. Slice the onions, carrots and garlic thinly into half moons and gently fry in a tablespoon of the olive oil until beginning to soften. Add the skinned and finely chopped tomatoes and fry for few minutes until they soften. Chop and add the parsley and cook for a further minute or two, reserving a few sprigs for garnish.

Rinse the lentils and transfer to a saucepan, covering with hot water. Bring to the boil and simmer gently until cooked but still whole. Don't add salt to the cooking water as it prevents the lentils from softening. Mix the lemon, oil, salt, and sugar. Drain the lentils and while warm add the lemon and oil dressing. Mix with the vegetables, and garnish with parsley, hard boiled egg quarters and red pepper flakes.

Barbunya Fasulye (Pinto beans with peppers)

200 grms dried pinto beans or 2 tins of haricot beans
3 carrots
2 onions
3 green or red peppers
4 tomatoes
2 cloves garlic
1 teaspoon sugar
1 tablespoon tomato puree
bunch of flat leafed or Italian parsley
1 teaspoon salt
3 tablespoons olive oil

Pinto beans are pink and white and make a pretty dish, but other white beans would work just as well. If using uncooked beans soak overnight, then cook for 40 minutes or until softening. Strain and discard the cooking water. Chop the vegetables. Heat the oil and add the onions, peppers and carrots frying until soft. Add the tomatoes and cook for a few minutes before adding a cup of water and the beans. Bring to the boil and simmer until the beans and vegetables are tender, add chopped parsley a few minutes before serving. Serve with side dishes of rice and yogurt.

Imam Bayıldı (The Imam Fainted – aubergine stuffed with tomatoes and peppers with olive oil)

Imam Bayıldı translates as 'the Priest Fainted' – the implication being that he fainted with pleasure! A second version of this tale is that he fainted at the cost of the olive oil used in the recipe.

    4 aubergines
    2 cups olive oil
    2 onions
    4 cloves garlic
    8 tomatoes
    1 bunch parsley
    2 green peppers
    1 teaspoon sugar
    salt and freshly ground pepper

This dish calls for the aubergines to be peeled in alternate lengthways strips – to give a striped effect. This helps the cooking process while holding the aubergine together. Make a slit to form a 'pocket' in the aubergine. Sprinkle generously with salt, cover with cold water, and set aside for 20 minutes. (I sometimes dispense with this traditional procedure when I'm in a hurry, and I haven't noticed much difference – but you may prefer to do it by the book.)

Finely chop the onions, garlic, tomatoes and parsley and add to gently warming olive oil in a frying pan. Season with salt and pepper. Fry gently for a few moments, before adding a few tablespoons of water, cover the pan and simmer for 10 minutes, or until the onions are soft.

Rinse the aubergines in cold water and pat dry with kitchen towel. Shallow fry the aubergines, turning in an inch or two of olive oil until they are lightly browned on all sides and beginning to soften. Remove with a slotted spoon and place in a baking dish open side up. Add the sliced green peppers to the pan and fry for a couple of minutes. (if you can acquire the long pepper variety, then cut them lengthways, otherwise cut a bell pepper into rings). Fill the aubergines with the tomato mixture, and lay a halved green pepper, or a few rings, on top. Drizzle the remaining olive oil over them, and add half a cup of water to the dish. Bake for 30 minutes in a moderate oven. Can be served hot or cold. This dish, although traditionally a starter, also makes a delicious main course served with rice and yogurt.

Ispanak ve Havuç (Spinach with carrots)

This is a lovely way to cook spinach, which brings out its full flavour, while adding a little sweetness with the addition of onions and carrots.

    500 grms spinach
    2 carrots
    2 onions
    2 cloves garlic
    grated nutmeg
    olive oil
    knob of butter

Finely slice the onions and garlic and cut the carrots into julienne strips. Sauté in the oil until softened. Add the washed and roughly chopped spinach. Add salt. Simmer gently removing from the heat before the spinach loses its colour. Dot with butter and grate nutmeg over before serving.

Patlıcan Puresi (Aubergine puree)

This creamy aubergine dish is a delicious accompaniment to any meal.

- **6 aubergines**
- **2 heaped tablespoons flour**
- **2 cups warm milk**
- **½ cup grated mature cheese**
- **4 tablespoons butter**
- **juice of half a lemon**
- **salt**
- **pepper**
- **nutmeg**

Prepare the aubergines by either grilling until the skin blisters and the flesh is soft, or bake in a hot oven for 20 minutes. Remove the skin and discard the stalks. Mash the cooked aubergine with the lemon juice and salt. Melt the butter and add the flour, stirring to make a roux. Slowly add the milk, stirring well until the sauce is smooth and creamy. Add the mashed aubergine and cook gently for 5 minutes. Add the cheese and grated nutmeg and heat through for a couple of minutes more. Serve hot.

Kızartma (Sauté Mediterranean vegetables in olive oil)

This dish shows how the simplest of recipes using good ingredients can be as delicious as more complicated dishes

- **4 medium potatoes**
- **3 aubergines**
- **8 long green peppers**
- **salt**
- **olive oil**
- **yogurt**
- **1 tablespoon butter**
- **1 teaspoon red pepper flakes**

Slice the aubergines and peppers lengthwise, and thinly 'chip' the potatoes. Using good quality olive oil shallow fry, starting with the potato chips and adding the aubergines and pepper strips after five minutes. Gently fry for ten minutes or until cooked and soft. Remove with a slotted spoon and drain on kitchen towel. Serve hot or cold – but best warm – covered in salted yogurt. Melt the butter and gently fry the red pepper for a minute, pour the red pungent mix over the yogurt dressing prior to serving. Eat with fresh bread chunks or with a plate of pilaf rice.

Yumurta Dolması

EGG DISHES

Yumurta Dolması (Stuffed Eggs)

4 eggs
½ small onion or a spring onion
Fresh dill
Fresh parsley
Juice of ½ lemon
3 tablespoons yogurt
3 tablespoons olive oil
red pepper flakes

Boil the eggs and remove the shell when cooled. Cut eggs lengthways and remove the yolks to a mixing bowl. Mash the yolks with the lemon juice, yogurt, salt and pepper. Slowly add the olive oil, mashing until the mix becomes soft. Stir in the very finely chopped ½ onion or the spring onion, and the finely chopped herbs. Fill the half egg whites with the mix and garnish with red pepper flakes.

Ispanakli Yumurta (Egg & Spinach Salad)

250 grms uncooked washed spinach, stems removed
1 small red onion
2 tomatoes
small bunch flat leafed parsley
2 hard-boiled eggs
100 grams crumbled feta cheese
Dressing
2 dessertspoons olive oil
4 dessertspoons lemon juice
½ teaspoon salt

Shred the washed spinach leaves in a bowl, or if small enough leave whole. Finely slice the red onion and dice the tomatoes, chop the parsley and combine with the spinach leaves. Finely chop the eggs, crumble the cheese and sprinkle over the ingredients in the bowl.

Whisk the oil, lemon and salt together, pour over the salad and toss, just prior to serving.

Ispanakli Yumurta (Poached eggs in spinach nests with pepper butter yogurt)

4 Eggs
500 grms spinach
2 medium onions
3 tablespoons butter
Turkish red pepper
Salt
1 cup yogurt

Finely slice and fry the onions in a tablespoon of the butter until soft. Wash, drain and finely chop the spinach and add to the pan. Stir until it wilts, but keeps its colour. Add the salt. Make wells in the spinach with a spoon, and break the eggs into the wells. Dot eggs and spinach with butter and cover with a lid. Reduce the heat and allow to cook gently until the egg whites become opaque.

Melt a spoon of the butter in a pan, add a teaspoon of red pepper and sauté for a minute until the butter is red. Lightly salt the yogurt, and pour it over the eggs and spinach. Finish by pouring the hot butter over the yogurt. Serve immediately.

Menemen (Turkish Scrambled Egg)

6 eggs
50 gms feta cheese
2 red or green peppers
1 large onion
4 large tomatoes (for this recipe you need fresh tomatoes - not tinned)
parsley
salt
pepper

Finely chop and fry the vegetables until they are soft and the juice from the tomatoes is partially reduced. Beat the eggs in a bowl, add pepper, salt and chopped parsley. Crumble the feta cheese into the mixture. Add to the pan and cook stirring constantly, taking care it does not become dry. Serve garnished with a sprinkle of red pepper. If you wish you can also add a few cubed pieces of spicy sausage or salami to this dish instead of cheese For a spicy version, which is also delicious, add a small teaspoon of red pepper flakes or chilli when you are frying the vegetables. Serve immediately with a crispy baguette.

Domates Dolması (Egg stuffed tomatoes)

8 large firm tomatoes
100 grms cheese (cheddar or feta)
2 teaspoons black pepper
4 eggs
half teaspoon salt
flat leafed Italian parsley

Cut the top of the tomato like a lid, remove inside of tomato, and reserve for another recipe. Mix the eggs in a bowl with the salt, fill tomatoes with egg mixture. Grate the cheese and mix with black pepper and parsley and sprinkle on egg mixture. Replace lid. Put on tray and put in the oven at 190 C for twenty minutes.

Çilbir (Poached eggs with garlic yogurt and pepper butter)

4 eggs (or as many as required)
1 tablespoon vinegar
salt
1-2 cloves of garlic
2 cups yogurt
1 tablespoon butter
½ teaspoon red pepper
salt

Add the vinegar to a pan of simmering water. Add the eggs one by one by breaking them into a cup and slowly lowering them into the water, keeping them as separate as possible. Remove after three minutes and place in a warmed serving dish. Beat the yogurt with salt and crushed garlic and pour over the eggs. Melt the butter and gently fry the red pepper or paprika for a minute, then drizzle over the yogurt. Serve with warm bread.

Nohutlu Makarna

PASTA DISHES

It is not commonly realized that the Turks had pasta long before Marco Polo introduced it to Italy following his travels in China. The Turks, originally from the steppes of Asia, long had contact with China, in fact a dialect of Turkish is still spoken in northwestern China. Pasta has been part of that inheritance, particularly the ravioli type parcels known as mantı, which are served with a yogurt sauce.

Nohutlu Makarna (Spicy chick pea pasta)

½ packet pasta (any shape)
1 onion
4 large tomatoes
1 dessertspoon tomato puree
2 garlic cloves
1 teaspoon red pepper (or ½ teaspoon chilli)
1 tin drained chickpeas
1 tablespoon olive oil
cup chopped parsley
salt
black pepper
pinch of sugar

Finely chop the onion and fry in the olive oil with the red pepper flakes. Remove the tomato skins by plunging in boiling water and then finely chop and add to the onions. Crush the garlic and add with the salt, pepper, sugar and chickpeas. Simmer gently until reduced. Stir in the tomato puree and cook another 2 minutes.

Add the pasta to a pan of boiling salted water and cook until soft but firm - al dente. Drain and mix with the sauce. Finely chop the parsley and stir through.

Cevizli Makarna (Spaghetti with walnuts)

This is a simple dish, easy to make and lovely with a green salad.

½ packet spaghetti
1 cup chopped walnuts
2 tablespoons butter
1 egg
parsley
salt
pepper

Cook the spaghetti in boiling salted water until soft but textured enough to 'feel' with the teeth – or al dente as the Italians say. Finely chop the walnuts and gently fry in the butter for a few minutes. Turn down the heat and add the drained spaghetti, beaten egg and salt and pepper and gently stir for another two minutes. Remove from heat, serve garnished with generous amount of chopped parsley.

Mantı (Ravioli dumplings with yogurt, pepper butter sauce and mint)

Tomato filling
- 8 good sized tomatoes
- 3 medium onions
- bunch flat leaf parley
- salt
- freshly ground black pepper

Remove the tomato skins by plunging them into boiling water. Chop the tomatoes, onions and parsley very finely and sauté in a little olive oil, salt and pepper until most of the water has evaporated and the mix is thick enough to be spooned onto the dough.

For the dough
- 400 grms white flour
- 1 egg
- 4 tablespoons water
- 1 teaspoon salt
- 4 cups vegetable stock

For the sauce
- 1 large pot of yogurt
- 2 - 4 crushed garlic cloves
- salt
- 3 tablespoons butter
- 1 – 2 teaspoon red pepper or paprika
- 1 teaspoon dried mint

To prepare the mantı sift the flour into bowl and add the egg, water, salt and knead on a well-floured surface. Leave to rest covered with a damp cloth for 1 hour. On the floured surface divide the dough in two, keeping one piece covered with the damp cloth while you work the other. Roll the dough as thinly as possible and then cut it into 6 cm (2 ½ inch) squares. Place a teaspoon of filling in the centre of the square, wet the edges of the dough and pick up the four corners squeezing them together. Arrange them in a well-oiled baking pan and bake in a moderate oven for around 20 minutes until the edges are lightly browned. Make up 4 cups of hot vegetable stock and pour over the mantı, cover and return to the oven. Continue cooking until all the stock is absorbed and the mantı are soft.

To make the sauce crush the garlic and add to the yogurt, with salt to taste. Pour over the cooked mantı. Melt the butter and gently fry the red pepper or paprika for a minute before drizzling over the mantı and yogurt. Sprinkle with dried mint and serve.

Pırasa Makarna (Baked leeks and macaroni with goats cheese and pine nuts)

½ packet macaroni
2-3 leeks
3 tablespoons olive oil or butter
1 heaped tablespoon pine nuts
1 egg
1 cup milk
salt
pepper
grated nutmeg
firm goats cheese or feta or any cheese or your choice

Cook the macaroni in boiling salted water until soft but textured enough to 'feel' with the teeth – or al dente as the Italians say. Heat the olive oil or butter (or half and half) and fry the washed and sliced leeks and pine nuts. Drain the macaroni and mix with the leeks, pine nuts and oil. Beat the egg with milk, add the salt pepper and grated nutmeg and pour onto the macaroni. Grease an oven dish and fill with the macaroni mix. Crumble the cheese of your choice into chunks and spread liberally over the macaroni. Bake for 25 – 30 minutes in a medium oven.

Domatesli Makarna (Baked tomato macaroni with olive oil and herbs)

½ packet macaroni
4 large tomatoes
2 onions
1 clove crushed garlic
1 tablespoon tomato puree
1 tablespoon lemon juice
3 tablespoons butter
1 tablespoon olive oil
1 tablespoons flour
2 cups milk
3 eggs
100 grms grated cheese
salt
black pepper
pinch of sugar
parsley to garnish

Cook the macaroni in boiling salted water until soft but textured enough to 'feel' with the teeth – or al dente as the Italians say. Remove the tomato skins by plunging in boiling water. Finely chop and sauté the tomatoes in olive oil with the crushed garlic and a pinch of sugar to create a sauce. Finely chop the onions and sauté in butter over a medium heat until soft, add the flour and fry a little longer until the flour smells nutty. Add the milk little by little stirring constantly to make a smooth sauce. Add salt, black pepper, the tomato garlic sauce, grated cheese and tomato puree. Stir well. Whisk the eggs in a basin and slowly add to the mix. Blend well. Drain the macaroni and mix with sauce. Butter an oven proof dish and fill with the macaroni mix. Bake in a medium oven until golden, about 30 – 40 minutes. Leave to rest for 5 minutes before turning out upside down onto a serving dish and garnishing with parsley.

Zeytinli Makarna (Spaghetti with capers and olives)

½ packet spaghetti
4 cloves crushed garlic
6 large tomatoes (or large tin tomatoes)
1 dessertspoon capers
1 tablespoon black olives
fresh basil leaves
olive oil
black pepper

Cook the spaghetti in boiling salted water until soft but textured enough to 'feel' with the teeth – or al dente as the Italians say. Crush the garlic and sauté in a tablespoon of olive oil. Add the peeled and finely chopped tomatoes and pepper. Season to taste. Simmer until the tomatoes reduce to a sauce. Add the capers, black olives and shredded basil leaves. Drain the spaghetti and add some olive oil, stirring to coat. Arrange in a dish and add the tomato sauce.

Limon Makarna (Lemon and herb tagliatelli)

Another simple pasta dish perfect for a summer lunch with green salad.

½ packet tagliatelli
2 tablespoons butter or olive oil
½ bunch parsley
½ bunch spring onions
1 teaspoon grated lemon rind
salt
freshly ground black pepper

Cook the tagliatelli in boiling salted water until soft but textured enough to 'feel' with the teeth – or al dente as the Italians say. Drain and add the melted butter or oil. Chop the parsley and onions and combine with the spaghetti and grated lemon rind. Serve with coarsely ground black pepper.

Peynirli Makarna (Basil and Feta Pasta Shells)

This is simple and delicious way to use pasta as either a hot dish or as a salad.

- ½ packet pasta shells
- 2 garlic cloves
- 2 tablespoons olive oil
- 1 tablespoon butter
- 150 grms feta cheese
- a handful of fresh basil leaves roughly torn or chopped
- a handful of black olives to garnish
- salt
- pul biber (red pepper flakes) optional

Crush the garlic and fry gently in the olive oil and butter until soft. Add the pasta shells to a large pan of boiling salted water and cook according to instructions.
Drain the shells, and pour the garlic butter/oil mix over. Crumble the feta, and tear the basil, mixing it with the pasta shells. Place on a serving dish and scatter with a handful of black olives and a sprinkle of Turkish red pepper or paprika.

Portakal Peltesi

DESSERTS

Turkey is famous for its very sweet, sticky, nutty pastries like baklava and for a variety of syrup soaked confectioneries. There are also creamy puddings, cakes made with yogurt or cheese and fruit compotes. However, it has to be said that while most Turkish food is supremely healthy, the desserts are nothing short of decadent, but are wonderful in small portions to just finish a meal. However, traditionally in Turkey desserts are eaten on their own in a pastahanesi, the Turkish version of a patisserie. (Those of an age to remember the hippy trail to India in the seventies will recall the famous Pudding Shop in Istanbul, which was the place to meet.) The usual practice is to serve fresh fruit after a meal.

Portakal Peltesi (Orange jelly with pistachios)

- 4 cups fresh orange juice
- 2 tablespoons cornstarch
- 4 dessertspoons sugar
- 2 oranges
- 2 tablespoons ground pistachios

Combine the juice, sugar, cornstarch and simmer, stirring constantly for 5 minutes. Peel and section the oranges, removing the translucent segment skins and any pith. Add to the mix and gently simmer for another 2 minutes. Divide among small serving bowls and chill. Sprinkle with ground pistachios before serving.

Irmik Helvası (Semolina Almond Helva with cinnamon)

- 250 grms semolina
- 125 grms butter
- 1 tablespoon blanched almonds
- 400 mls milk
- 200 grms sugar
- ¼ teaspoon ground cinnamon

Melt the butter, add the semolina and almonds and stir over a low heat until lightly browned. Add the milk and cinnamon, and simmer until completely absorbed. Stir in the sugar. Allow to cool before serving.

Şekerpare (Syrup soaked almond cakes)

These little cakes are softened in syrup making them absolutely a decadent treat, but are lovely on their own too, warm from the oven with a spoon of yogurt, cream or crème fraiche.

 120grms butter
 2 cups white flour
 ½ teaspoon baking powder
 pinch salt
 ½ cup caster sugar
 1 tablespoon semolina
 1 tablespoon ground almonds
 2 eggs
 Blanched almonds

For the syrup

 1 cup sugar
 1 cup water
 juice of half a lemon

Blend the sugar and butter in a bowl, adding 1 beaten egg with the flour, baking power, semolina and ground almonds. Knead the mixture until it form a smooth paste. Make small walnut size balls of the mixture, using a little butter on your hands to prevent sticking. Place on a greased baking sheet, slightly flatten the balls, then press a blanched almond into the centre of each one. Brush with beaten egg yolk and bake at 180 C for 25 – 30 minutes.
The next bit is optional, but the syrup does make the cake deliciously moist and sweet. To make the syrup bring the sugar and water to the boil, then simmer uncovered for 15 minutes. Add the lemon juice and allow to cool. Cut the cake into squares, pour over the syrup and refrigerate. Serve chilled with cream and guilty pleasure.

Zerde (Saffron Rice with pomegranate)

This pudding is traditionally served at weddings, and to make a more luxurious and exotic version rose water is used to flavour it.

 125 grms pudding rice
 6 cups water (or milk)
 2 tablespoons rose water (optional)
 ½ - 1 cup sugar (according to taste)
 1 tablespoon of arrowroot (or cornflour)
 2 pinches saffron
 1 pomegranate

Rinse the rice and place in a heavy bottomed pan with the water and sugar, and simmer for 25 minutes, or until soft. Add the saffron. Mix the arrowroot with a little water and then add to the rice and cook for a further 20 minutes until thickened. Divide the rice into small bowls and allow to cool. Remove the pomegranate seeds. A tip is to slice the fruit in half and hold it over a mixing bowl while beating the outer skin with a rolling pin or heavy spoon. This removes the seeds with surprising ease, leaving the bitter pith. Garnish the saffron coloured puddings with the bright red seeds. You can also sprinkle some currants and pine nuts should you wish.

Zerde

Muz Tatlısı (Bananas with walnuts, butter and orange sauce)

This is a simple but delicious dish, always a firm favourite

**6 bananas
juice of 1 lemon
1 tablespoon butter
2 tablespoons honey
cup of orange juice
½ cup crushed walnuts**

Peel the bananas and pour over the lemon juice. Melt the butter in a frying pan and add the bananas and lemon juice. Fry on each side until browning, and then add the honey, orange juice and crushed walnuts. Simmer until bananas are soft and orange juice is reduced. Serve warm with yogurt or cream.

Alternatively follow the same procedure, but instead of simmering, bake in a medium oven for 25 minutes

Revani (Pistachio Semolina Cake)

**125 grms plain flour
150 grms semolina
50 grms sugar
1 teaspoon vanilla extract
8 medium eggs
1 tablespoon lemon zest
50 grms ground pistachio nuts (remove the red skins if grinding them yourself)**

For the syrup

**1 cup sugar
1 cup water
2 tablespoons lemon juice**

Separate the eggs. Beat the yolks with the sugar, vanilla and lemon zest. Fold in the flour, semolina and ground pistachio nuts, reserving some pistachio to decorate
Whisk the egg whites into stiff peaks, and then gently fold into the mixture.
Pour into a 12 x 15 x 2 inch baking tin, lightly buttered and floured. Bake in a moderate oven for 30 - 40 minutes, until golden brown.

The next bit is optional, but the syrup does make the cake deliciously moist.
To make the syrup bring the sugar and water to the boil, then simmer uncovered for 15 minutes. Add the lemon juice and allow to cool. Cut the cake into squares, pour over the syrup, sprinkle with ground pistachio, and refrigerate. Serve chilled with cream and guilty pleasure. You can replace the syrup with yogurt or crème fraiche for a healthier alternative.

Bülbül Yuvası (Nightingale nests)

This is a variation of baklava, which is easy to make and has a lovely name!

12 sheets filo pastry
1 cup melted butter
2 cups of finely ground walnuts
½ cup ground pistachio nuts
whole pistachios

For the syrup

1 cup sugar
1 cup water
juice of half a lemon

To make the syrup bring the sugar and water to the boil, then simmer uncovered for 15 minutes. Add the lemon juice and allow to cool.

Take a sheet of filo, working with the longest edge of the pastry next to you and brush to the edges with melted butter and sprinkle with walnuts. Roll up into a long tube, and then coil into nest shapes. Repeat with each sheet. Pack the nests onto a baking sheet so they touch. Brush well with melted butter and bake for around 30 minutes or until golden brown at 180C. Add half the syrup and return to the oven for a further 5 minutes. Pour the remaining syrup over and leave to cool. Cover with ground pistachios and place two or three whole pistachios as 'eggs' in the nests.

Yoğurt Tatlısı (Yogurt cake)

250 grms thick yogurt
350 grms caster sugar
300 grms flour
1 tablespoon butter
3 eggs
½ teaspoon baking powder

For the syrup

1 cup sugar
1 cup water
juice and grated zest of half a lemon

To make the syrup bring the sugar and water to the boil, then simmer uncovered for 15 minutes. Add the lemon juice and allow to cool.

Beat the sugar into the yogurt, add the beaten eggs, melted butter, flour and baking powder and mix well. Pour into an greased baking tray so the mix is about 2 inches deep, and bake at 190C for 40 minutes, or until golden brown. Pour the syrup over and allow to cool. Cut into squares and serve. Omit the syrup if you prefer and serve with a spoon of honey yogurt.

Muhallebi (Classic milk pudding with cinnamon)

4 cups milk
3 tablespoons rice flour
2 tablespoons cornflour
2 - 3 tablespoons sugar

Add some of the milk gradually to the rice flour, cornflour and sugar, mixing to make a runny paste. Bring the remaining milk to the boil and add slowly to the flour paste, whisking well. Return the mix to the pan, stirring continuously until it thickens. Pour into individual dishes and allow to set. Serve chilled, dusted with cinnamon. The simple sweet and creamy flavour lends itself to any topping if you prefer – grated coconut, ground pistachios or cocoa. It is also lovely with a few spoons of poached fruit or a spoonful of runny morello cherry jam.

Kayısı Tatlısı (Stuffed apricots with cream and pistachios)

250 grms dried apricots
juice of ½ lemon
1 cup of water
1 cup sugar
100 grms clotted cream or cheese
pistachios

Soak the dried apricots overnight in water. Drain and add to the water, sugar and lemon juice. Poach gently until the apricots soften, but not so much that they fall apart, and the syrup thickens. Remove the apricots and allow to cool. Stuff with clotted cream, or for a sweet and sour variation, which I prefer, use cheese – I particularly like the zing of feta. Press a green pistachio nut into the cream/cheese. Arrange on a plate and pour over the syrup. You can omit the syrup if you want to watch the calories.

Incir Tatlısı (Stuffed figs with cream and walnuts)

250 grms dried figs
juice of ½ lemon
1 cup of water
1 cup sugar
100 grms clotted cream or cheese
walnuts

Follow the same process as for the apricots above.

Kayısı Tatlısı

Kadin Göbeği (Lady's navel)

There are three enchantingly named desserts made from the same mix, but shaped differently - Kadin Göbeği (Lady's Navel), Dilber Dudağı (Beauty's Lips) and Vezir Parmağı (Vizier's Fingers) – names redolent with echoes of the Sultan's court and harem.

250 grms white flour
100 grms butter
3 eggs
pinch salt
1 cup water
sunflower oil for frying

For the syrup

1 cup sugar
1 cup water
juice of half a lemon

To make the syrup bring the sugar and water to the boil, then simmer uncovered for 15 minutes. Add the lemon juice and allow to cool.

Melt the butter, add the flour and salt and gently fry. Slowly add the water, beating with a wooden spoon to create a dough. If necessary add a little more water, and cook for a few minutes stirring constantly. Allow to cool. Add the beaten eggs and knead for ten minutes. Using a little oil on your hands, take large walnut sized pieces and roll into balls. Press them lightly to flatten, and then make the 'navel' with your finger. Drop the 'navels' into the oil over a medium heat and fry gently until golden brown. Don't put too many in the pan at once. Remove and drain well on kitchen paper, before dropping into the syrup. Leave to absorb the syrup for fifteen minutes before removing.

To make Beauty's Lips repeat the above process, flattening the balls into rounds and folding in two to create 'lips' – fry as before. For Vizier's Fingers do the same, rolling the mix into finger shapes.

Elma Tatlısı (Baked apples with cinnamon and walnuts)

4 dessert apples
2 cups orange juice
4 tablespoons honey
½ cup chopped walnuts
½ cup soaked raisins
butter
½ teaspoon ground cinnamon

Soak the raisins and walnuts in a cup of the orange juice until swollen. Peel the apples in a spiral to create a striped effect. Core. Drain the raisins and walnuts and fill the apples. Place in an ovenproof dish and dot with butter. Heat the orange juice with the honey and cinnamon, and pour over the apples. Bake at 180C until apples are soft.

Remove apples. Pour juice into a pan and thicken with a teaspoon of cornflour, cooking until it thickens. Pour over the apples and serve warm or cold with yogurt or cream.

Lor Tatlısı (Semolina Cheese Cake)

400 grms feta cheese (If the cheese is very salty soak it in cold water for a couple of hours)
2 tablespoons butter
3 tablespoons sugar
2 tablespoons flour
2 tablespoons semolina
½ teaspoon baking powder
4 egg yolks

1 cup water
1 cup sugar
2 tablespoons lemon juice

Beat the sugar with the egg yolks. Melt the butter, and when cool, add to the egg mix with the mashed cheese. Mix well. Add the flour, semolina and baking powder mixing well. Take egg sized pieces, roll into a ball and then flatten into rounds. Place on an oiled baking sheet and bake in a medium hot oven for 20 –25 minutes, until golden brown.

Make a syrup by boiling the water, sugar and lemon juice for 15 minutes. Pour over the cakes and bake for a further 15 minutes in a low oven. Allow to cool before serving.

Huzur Vadisi dinner bell

Index

DESSERTS 61

Baked apples with cinnamon and walnuts 68
Bananas with walnuts, butter and orange sauce 64
Classic milk pudding with cinnamon 66
Lady's navel 68
Nightingale nests 65
Orange jelly with pistachios 61
Pistachio Semolina Cake 64
Saffron Rice with pomegranate 62
Semolina Almond Helva with cinnamon 61
Semolina Cheese Cake 69
Stuffed apricots with cream and pistachios 66
Stuffed figs with cream and walnuts 66
Syrup soaked almond cakes 62
Yogurt cake 65

EGG DISHES 51

Egg & Spinach Salad 51
Egg stuffed tomatoes 53
Poached eggs in spinach nests with pepper butter yogurt 52
Poached eggs with garlic yogurt and pepper butter 53
Stuffed Eggs 51
Turkish Scrambled Egg 53

MAIN DISHES 39

Aromatic herbed spiced rice with currants for stuffing vegetables 43
Aubergine pilav 41
Aubergine puree 49
Aubergine stuffed with tomatoes and peppers with olive oil 48
Bean Pilaki with Tarator Sauce 45
Bulgur pilav with vegetables 40

Bulgur with crushed walnuts and fresh herbs 39
Green lentils with lemon dressing 47
Istanbul Pilav 42
Izmir Pilav 43
Lemon Rice 41
Lentil rissoles 45
Pinto beans with peppers 47
Rice stuffed tomatoes 43
Sauté Mediterranean vegetables in olive oil 49
Spicy tomato bulgur with parsley and currants 39
Spinach with carrots 48
Stuffed bell peppers 44
Tarator Sauce 45

PASTA DISHES 55

Baked leeks and macaroni with goats cheese and pine nuts 57
Baked tomato macaroni with olive oil and herbs 57
Basil and Feta Pasta Shells 59
Lemon and herb tagliatelli 58
Ravioli dumplings with yogurt, pepper butter sauce and mint 56
Spaghetti with capers and olives 58
Spaghetti with walnuts 55
Spicy chick pea pasta 55

SALADS and APPETIZERS 21

Aubergine Fritters with Yogurt 27
Aubergine Salad with Yogurt 21
Aubergine stuffed with tomatoes & peppers with olive oil 29
Beetroot and Tahini Salad 32
Broad Bean Paté 33
Butter Bean and Red Onion Salad 30
Canellini Bean Salad 34
Carrot yogurt salad with tahini and walnuts 22
Cauliflower, sesame and lemon salad 30
Cheese Stuffed Mushrooms with crispy breadcrumb topping 33

Chickpea, Sesame, Garlic and Lemon Dip   27
Courgette, Feta and Dill Fritters   27
Crispy batter carrots and yogurt   23
Deep fried cheese stuffed aubergines   35
Feta cheese and herb filo parcels   26
Garlic Cucumber Yogurt   31
Green beans in olive oil and tomato sauce   33
Leek and walnut fritters   35
Pea, apple and mint salad   30
Potato Salad with boiled eggs and black olives   31
Purslane and garlic yogurt with pepper butter sauce   36
Purslane salad with garlic and lemon   23
Red cabbage salad   22
Rocket, garlic, feta and sesame seed salad   29
Shepherd's Salad   22
Spicy tomato, pepper and cucumber dip   34
Toast Salad   23
Tomato and basil salad   26
Vine leaves stuffed with cinnamon, pine nut and currant rice   36

SOUPS 13

Bride's Soup   14
Courgette Soup   18
Flour Soup   16
Mushroom Soup   19
Potato Soup   13
Rice Soup   16
Summer – Winter Soup   15
Tomato Soup   17
Turkish lentil soup   15
Wedding Soup with sour sauce   18
Yogurt soup   14

Printed in Great Britain
by Amazon